BULLDOGS
TODAY

Chris Thomas

RINGPRESS

RINGPRESS

Published by Ringpress Books Ltd,
PO Box 8, Lydney, Gloucestershire GL15 6YD.

Discounts available for bulk orders
Contact the Special Sales Manager at
the above address. Telephone 01594 563800.

ISBN 1 86054 005 8

Printed and bound in Singapore
by Kyodo Printing Co.

CONTENTS

4

To my mother, Emily Grace Jenkins

ACKNOWLEDGEMENTS

Firstly, I would like to thank my mother for all her help during my early years in this most difficult of breeds. Whether sharing in the two-hourly regime of feeding young puppies, or helping to keep spirits high when the kennel suffered what seemed to be a severe setback, she was always there. I would also like to thank my partner, Graham, for his support during the writing of this book.

Bulldoggers from overseas, whose contributions have helped enormously, include: my good friends, Ove Germundsson, from Sweden; Helena and Ari Hyvonen for their extensive research on the breed in Finland; Ann van Heuvel for tracing the Bulldog's history in Holland; George and Julia van Rooyen for their comprehensive information on the breed in South Africa; Helene Denis for her help on the Bulldog in France; Howard Randell for his informed contribution covering the Bulldog scene in Australia; Joan Railton-Wilson for her recollections and photographs of the breed's development in Canada; and last but not least, Bob and Susan Rodenski for their help in writing about the Bulldog in the USA.

My grateful thanks to John and Maggie Story for all their help, and to the Bulldog Club Inc. for allowing me to use the line drawings by J. Hay-Hutchison to illustrate the Breed Standard.

Thanks must also go to Julia Barnes and Ann Smiley of Ringpress Books for their help and advice throughout.

All of the prints and paintings used as illustrations in this book are from my own collection.

CHRIS THOMAS

INTRODUCTION

My grandmother was from a farming background and I spent many evenings as a child listening to her reminiscences about life around the farm. But, more importantly to me, was her involvement with the world of showing. As market gardeners, the agricultural show scene played an important part in family life, and the exhibiting of garden produce, as well as cattle, pigs and poultry, was a major part of running a successful farm, if demand for stock was to be maintained. Before my father's untimely death, my parents were keen exhibitors of Ermine Rex rabbits, and I have vague recollections of attending shows with them at the local Drill Hall.

The love of animals I inherited from my parents and grandparents has stayed with me. I have exhibited various livestock, including cagebirds, poultry, cats and goats, although my greatest enjoyment has come from breeding and exhibiting pedigree dogs.

In 1965 I acquired my first show dog, a Rough Collie, whom I loved dearly. However, there was a breed, the Bulldog, that I had seen occasionally at shows – and soon I became absolutely captivated. In 1974 I celebrated my twenty-first birthday, and I saw this as the golden opportunity for making public my ambition to own a Bulldog. After months of searching, culminating in a visit to the Bulldog Club Centenary Show, I was lucky enough to find what I had been searching for. Later that year, Chiansline White Regality came to live with us.

Pica, as she was christened, was white and red; she had a super temperament and was nicely bred. Her breeders were John and Sheila Alcock, who lived close to us. At that time, Sheila was secretary of the London Bulldog Society, and had been editor of the club's magazine, *The Bulldog Broadsheet*, for twenty years. During my early years in the breed, I probably spent as much time at John and Sheila's home as I did at my own. But they never seemed to tire of my relentless questions regarding Bulldogs, often involving delving through piles of old books and pedigrees until the information was found.

Pica formed the foundation of the Kingrock kennel, and there is not a Bulldog carrying this affix anywhere in the world that does not trace its pedigree back to her. In 1976 Pica was mated to George and Eva Parker's famous Champion, Brumigum Stroller Boy of the Regions, and from this litter, I kept a red and white bitch, Kingrock My-Nora-Tee. Although

Chiansline White Regality of Kingrock: Bred by John and Sheila Alcock. The foundation bitch of the Kingrock kennel – all Kingrock Bulldogs worldwide have this bitch in their pedigree.

Ch. Kingrock Freezo: An outstanding sire for the Kingrock kennel.

not an outstanding show specimen, she still managed to win moderately well, and she was as sound as a bell. However, it was as a brood that she was to show her full potential.

In 1979 My-Nora-Tee was mated to Pat Dellar's Merriveen Son of Satan, producing a litter of four puppies – two dogs and two bitches. One of the bitches went to the stud owner in lieu of a stud fee, and one of the dogs was retained. Both became Champions. The bitch won many top awards, including Bulldog of the Year, and seventeen Challenge Certificates, including Crufts. The dog, Ch. Kingrock Captain Christian, did not aspire to the dizzy heights of his sister, but he sired some of the top-winning stock around at the time, including the famous Ch. Ocobo Skipper.

My-Nora-Tee was later mated to a Son of Satan son, Ch. Merriveen Happy Daze, and this litter contained an eye-catching white dog puppy, who went on to become the outstanding stud, Ch. Kingrock Freezo. Freezo, mated to a daughter of Captain Christian, Kingrock and Roll, produced four puppies. The two dog puppies in this litter both went on to become Champions. One of these was the well-known Ch. Kingrock Canis Pugnax, who died in 1993 at the age of ten. He was a great character and is sadly missed around the kennel. Many items depicting a head study of him have been produced over the years, such as ring-clips, brooches, tie-pins, plates, tea services, table lamps, wall plaques, clocks, etc.

Canis Pugnax was mated to Kingrock Katrina, litter-sister to Freezo. The resulting litter included a beautiful red and white dog puppy who went on to become the international Champion featured on this book's jacket. Buster has produced Champion offspring at home and abroad, and he is the sire of Kingrock's two most recent Champions.

There are many Bulldogs who have contributed to the success of the kennel, and although it tends to be the stud dogs who are most often in the limelight, there is a lot of truth in the old adage that "the strength of a kennel lies in its bitches". I have seldom shown bitches, but the kennel owes a lot to the broods, without whom there would be no promising youngsters waiting in the wings.

I have bred Champions in French Bulldogs and Boston Terriers, but there will never be another breed to compare with the Bulldog. I have been fortunate enough to judge the breed in many countries, including Sweden, France, Switzerland, Norway, Spain, Holland and Finland, which has been a great honour and privilege.

Chapter One

EARLY HISTORY OF THE BULLDOG

Much of the history of this unique and fascinating breed is buried in the mists of time and, although documentary evidence about its development is available, it is not always easy to distinguish between what is fact and what is fiction. Few breeds can have created as much folklore as the Bulldog.

THE MYTHS

Many legends have evolved over the centuries. To illustrate this I have selected an extract from *The Annals of the Knights of St John of Jerusalem* which contains an account of the appearance of an enormous serpent on the Island of Rhodes in the fifteenth century: "which reptile caused widespread devastation and also mortality to human beings, flocks and herds. A number of the Knights one after another lost their lives in attempting to destroy the serpent, until there arose one Deodati de Gozona, who hit upon an ingenious method of combatting the serpent. He caused to be constructed an artificial replica of the creature and then secured 'twelve Bulldogs of the true breed'." By some means the movements of the living monster were reproduced in the dummy and the dogs were trained for two years to attack it. The training period ended, Deodati repaired to the monster's den with his twelve dogs. The first round went to the serpent, for five of the dogs were destroyed with one blow. Deodati, however, then inflicted a severe lance wound upon the face of the serpent, which, according to the account, was so much annoyed that he 'hissed dreadfully' and rearing up, 'appeared like a tall beech stripped of its branches'. The sight was too much for the Knight's horse, who threw his rider and fled. The dismounted Knight stood his ground while the remaining dogs set about the serpent, and between them the creature received many wounds. The fight, however, had now been going on for three hours, and Deodati was reaching the point of exhaustion, when one of his dogs, named Dreadnought, managed to get his teeth in the serpent's throat and to remain hanging there until Deodati was able to administer the final blow. The incident closed with a triumphal procession through the island, headed by the skin of the serpent, carried before Dreadnought the Bulldog.

In this case it is fairly safe to assume that the story is purely mythical. But it is not always so easy to separate fact from fiction.

FIRST APPEARANCES IN LITERATURE

The first mention of the Bulldog in English literature occurs in 1500 and, over the centuries, many written works refer to the breed although, rather confusingly, not always by this name.

Several terms were used to describe the forerunner of the Bulldog, which had been kept for a variety of purposes, either as a guard, or as a butcher's dog to help in the control of unruly oxen, or as a hunting dog for boar. But perhaps the most common use, and it was certainly the purpose for which the breed attained notoriety, was for the so-called 'sport' of baiting.

One of the earliest terms, which is still occasionally seen in use today, is "Bandogge". This description is first used by Dr Caius, a physician to Elizabeth I, in 1576. The author William Harrison, in his *Description of England* 1586, attributes this name to the fact that "manie of them are tied up in chaines and strong bonds in the daie time for doing hurt abroad, which is an huge dog, stubborn, ouglie, eager, burthenouse of bodie (and therefore of little swiftness), terrible and fearful to behold, and oftentimes more fierce and fell than anie Archadian or Corsican cur."

Shakespeare mentions them in *King Henry VI* act 1: "The time when screech owls and Bandogges howl and spirits walk and ghosts break up their graves." In *The Merry Wives of Windsor*, Shakespeare mentions a bear called "Sackerson" who had achieved notoriety, no doubt, for his victories in the baiting ring.

Shakespeare used the then familiar term 'Bandogge', whereas his friend, the poet and playwright Ben Jonson, in his play *The Silent Woman*, first acted in 1609, mentions both Bulldogs and Beardogs. This is believed to be the earliest reference to the breed with the spelling as it is common today.

ANCESTRY

There is still much discussion and debate about the breed's exact ancestry; but it is now generally agreed that the Bulldog and the Mastiff had the Allaunt as their forerunner – although it is recognised that the term Mastiff was applied indiscriminately to all kinds of large dogs and would have included those also referred to as Bulldogs. The same is true of the name Bandogge, which was not originally applied to a distinct variety but to those dogs who spent most of their lives chained up or, as it was called in those early days, 'bound'. An anonymous writer stated in 1707: "Our Mastiffs, especially those we call Bulldogs, are of unmatchable courage."

BULL-BAITING

This became popular in England during the early part of the thirteenth century. It was preceded, some two hundred years earlier, by bear-baiting. History tells us that on St Brice's day, November 13th 1209, Earl Warren, then Lord of Stamford, while looking down from his castle, observed an enraged bull being tormented by a pack of butcher's dogs which then chased the terrified creature through the town: "This sight so pleased the Earl, that he gave the castle meadow, where the bull's combat began, for a common to the butchers of the town, after the first grass was mowed, on condition that they should find a 'mad bull' on a day six weeks before Christmas for the continuance of that sport for ever."

'The Baited Bull Broke Loose', published 1802. During the bait the bull wore a heavy collar and was secured by a strong rope approximately four yards in length.

'Bull Broke Loose': Bulldogs were trained to approach their adversary head-on, keeping as close to the ground as possible in order to avoid the bull's horns.

This 'sport' soon became popular and by the end of the thirteenth century most English market towns had their own 'Bull-Ring', and at Tutbury in Staffordshire annual baitings continued for five centuries until brought to an end by the intervention of the then Duke of Devonshire in 1778.

It was different to 'Bull running', where the bull was not tethered but pursued through the town by dogs and those wishing to join in the chase; but this pastime was not as popular as baiting and it is believed that Bull-running was practised in just three English towns.

The bull-bait was a far more manageable affair, attracting a large following in virtually every town throughout the land and patronised by people from all classes.

During the bait the bull was made to wear a heavy collar which was secured to a stout rope of approximately four yards in length. This was attached at its other end to a stake or large metal ring fixed firmly in the ground. The term Bullring applied both to the arena and to the ring to which the unfortunate creature was secured. In the early days it was widely believed that baiting the bull tenderised the meat and it was not unknown for some boroughs to have by-laws decreeing that any butcher who slaughtered a bull before it had been baited in the market place would be liable to pay a fine.

> "What creature that, so fierce and bold,
> That springs and scorns to leave his hold?,
> It is the Bulldog, matchless, brave,
> Like Britons on the swelling wave."
> "The Bull Bait" *Sporting Anecdotes*, Pierce Egan, 1820.

The Bulldogs' main objective during the bait was the "pinning and holding" of the bull. For this purpose the dogs used were trained to approach their adversary head on, while keeping as near to the ground as possible, thus lessening the chance of being tossed by the bull's horns. When within range, the Bulldog would spring in an attempt to secure a hold on the fleshy part of the bull's nose, thereby pinning his adversary to the ground. Of course it was not unusual for a minor error in judgement to result in the Bulldog falling victim to the menacing horns and being tossed thirty or forty feet into the air.

> "Raised to the clouds the sprawling Mastiffs fly,
> And add new monsters to the frighted sky."
> Sir Richard Blackmore (early 18th Century)

Sand was often used to surround the ring in the vain hope that it would break the fall of the less fortunate contestants. Those watching would also try to catch the dog in an attempt to limit the damage caused by the fall and speed a return to the bait.

> "The clamorous youth to aid each other call,
> On their broad backs to break their favourite's fall."
> Sir Richard Blackmore

As an early writer observed: "unless perhaps some active dame can intercept him in her outstretched apron (as was the custom in certain parts of Devonshire and Staffordshire), the animal would indeed suffer a 'damnable squelch'."

In the event of some damage befalling the dog before the bait was complete, emergency first aid would be carried out at the ringside. This would include the sewing of open wounds and, in the case of broken limbs, splints fitted to enable a continuation of the contest.

We now regard bull-baiting as a barbaric and callous pastime but it should be remembered that many of the characteristics so admired in the Bulldog of today have descended from those early days in the bullring – the short muzzle with its 'laid-back' nose to enable the dog to breath whilst holding onto the bull's fleshy nose; the wide upturned underjaw which gives a vice-like grip; the head-furrows to channel away the bull's blood from the eyes and nose during the pinning of the bull, which could last for some time; the heavy front and shoulder

'Tumbler', owned by Ben White, and 'Bess', owned by Lady Sandwich, baiting a bull belonging to Bill Gibbons. From a painting by J.C. Scanlan, circa 1836.

Bear baiting: Bears, monkeys, badgers, asses, horses, and even lions were considered fair game.

In Warwickshire, 1825, several Bulldogs were killed and many more were badly injured in an attempt to bait lions belonging to George Wombell.

to give some degree of stability; and the temperament that we still see today of steady determination and great courage, especially with regard to pain, for which the breed seemingly has an incredibly high threshold. An account in the *Sporting Magazine* of 1824 illustrates this: "A butcher brought a bitch accompanied by her litter of puppies to a bull-bait. Upon letting the bitch loose, the butcher exclaimed, 'Now gentlemen, I will say nothing of the goodness of this breed; you will see.' Although she had scarcely a tooth in her head, the bitch immediately pinned the bull. The butcher then cut her to pieces with a hedge-bill, and she only quitted her hold with her last breath. There was instantly a great demand for her puppies which the butcher sold for five guineas apiece."

It was not only the unfortunate bull that was used in this barbaric way: bears, monkeys, badgers, asses, horses, lions and various other animals were all considered fair game. There is an account of a visit in 1623 by the Spanish Ambassador to the Bankside Bear Gardens, located within the Paris Gardens, Southwark, which contained one of London's most famous baiting arenas. It was said that the Spanish ambassador was delighted with the proceedings "where they showed him all the pleasures they could, both with bull, horse and bear, besides jack-asses and apes. They then turned a white bear into the Thames where the dogs baited him while swimming, which was the best sport of all."

The Paris Garden was not only the place of suffering for animals, as an account by Prynne, in his *Histriomastix* of 1632 illustrates. "On Sunday 13th January of that year, during a bait, the overloaded scaffolding supporting the crowds collapsed. Five men and two women were killed outright and more than one hundred and fifty injured, many of whom died shortly after." At the time this was seen by some as retribution for holding the event on a Sunday. There is no surprise in the fact that it seems not to have been considered possible that the retribution could have been for holding the bait at all; it was simply seen by many as a sign from heaven that Sunday was not a suitable day for such fun and frivolity. Indeed the 'sport' of baiting was staunchly, and in some cases passionately, followed by a large percentage of the population and maintained its popularity for more than six hundred years.

LANGUAGE FROM THE PAST

Terminology still in common use today has its roots buried in the breed's chequered past – some, for example, from the barbarous sport of dog fighting, which became more popular in the eighteen hundreds following the abolition of baiting. These contests were normally carried out in a circular pit with either an earth or a sawdust floor-covering. Before the fight began a line was scratched in the floor surface, or a piece of string tied across the centre of the ring, termed the scratch. The dogs were then placed in the pit and would fight until one turned away. They were then attended to by their seconds, who would prepare them for the next 'round' when time was called. The dogs were sent in turn across the ring to attack their opponent and this procedure continued until either, through sheer exhaustion the fight was declared a draw, or one of the contestants was killed outright, or a dog refused to cross the line to fight – he did not "come up to scratch".

Another phrase still in common use, again a descendant from the dog-fighting pits, comes from the scurrilous act of spreading some foul-tasting concoction into the dog's coat just prior to the fight to discourage the opposition from securing a hold. In an attempt to stop this

*The early Bulldogs:
'Crib and Rosa',
painted by A. Cooper,
engraved by John
Scott, published 1817.*

malpractice the fight organisers would employ someone to 'taste' the dogs, which entailed the licking over of the entire body of the dog. Those that had been tampered with would be disqualified, and these dogs were said to have been 'licked'.

The terms 'top dog' and 'bottom dog' were used to describe the contestant's position in the pit and, although the fight was usually to the death, an owner who wished to withdraw his dog had the option of throwing in the towel. I wonder how many of us who use these expressions have ever stopped to wonder how they first came about?

In 1802 a bill to abolish bull-baiting was thrown out of the House of Commons after much heated debate. Finally in 1835 the practices of Bull and Bear baiting and dog fighting were made illegal by an Act of Parliament, although in reality baitings were not to stop for some years to come. Eccles in Lancashire was celebrated for its baitings until 1840 and they continued at West Derby until 1853.

> "The mongrel's hold will slip,
> But only crowbars loose the Bulldog's grip,
> Small though he looks, the jaw that never yields,
> Drags down the bellowing monarch of the fields."
>
> O. Wendell Holmes   (1809-1894)

EARLY DESCRIPTIONS OF THE BREED

A description of the Bulldog written by Captain Thomas Brown FRSE in 1829, shortly before the abolition of baiting, in his book *Anecdotes of Dogs* says: "His head is broad, his nose short and the under-jaw projects beyond the upper, which gives him a fierce and disagreeable aspect. His eyes are distant and prominent and have a peculiar suspicious-like leer, which, with the distension of his nostrils, gives him also a contemptuous look; and

ABOVE: 'Jem Burns' Pets', painted by L. Booth in 1844. This is of particular historical interest, depicting the youthful Jack Shepherd (later to gain notoriety for his highway exploits) with Bulldogs Duchess, Cribb and Ball, the property of Jem Burns of prize-fighting fame.

LEFT: 'On Guard', an oil painting by Robert Taylor, dated 1871.

from his teeth being always seen, he has the constant appearance of grinning while he is perfectly placid. He is the most ferocious and unrelenting of the canine tribe and may be considered courageous beyond every other creature in the world, for he will attack any animal whatever be his magnitude. The Bulldog is one of the original and peculiar races of Britain, and may be ranked in point of originality with the shepherd's dog and Irish Greyhound. In various districts of England this breed is still preserved in its native purity, by that class of people who delight in bull-baiting and fighting of dogs; both of which amusements, alike inhuman, are now happily on the decline. But Bulldogs are not so numerous as they were, nor so carefully attended to, in consequence of the decline of what was anciently a favourite sport. At a former period great numbers were purchased and transported to other countries, for which enormous prices were sometimes given."

The great author of dog books, who wrote under the name Stonehenge, said of the Bulldog that: "in brute courage and unerring tenacity of purpose he stands unrivalled among quadrupeds....I believe that every breed of dog possessed of very high courage owes it to a cross with the Bulldog. He is not only the most courageous dog, but the most courageous animal in the world."

Not all writers on the breed were quite as kind: "The Bulldog is scarcely capable of any education and is fitted for nothing but combat and ferocity." *Bulldogs and All About Them* , 1825.

With such critics – what of the Bulldog after the abolition of baiting?

Chapter Two

RECENT HISTORY

Although the Bulldog had many enthusiasts, the abolition of baiting brought with it a decline in the breed's popularity and several types of crossbred Bulldogs started to appear as demand for a "working" Bulldog no longer existed.

By the mid eighteen hundreds the Pug had been introduced into some lines, bringing the size down drastically and shortening the muzzle still further, which many considered desirable. Also terrier blood had been introduced to improve the Bulldog's agility.

The larger Spanish bulldogs, which had an average weight of between ninety and one hundred and twenty pounds, were being imported by breeders who felt that the breed had lost some of its power and substance during the latter part of the eighteen hundreds. One such breeder, Mr F. Adcock, introduced from Spain an immense dog named Toro who weighed around ninety pounds. As a stud dog Toro proved to be a great disappointment and his progeny lacked the attributes of their sire.

A description of Toro appeared in *The Field* publication: "a massive dark chestnut or 'carroty' brindled dog, with blackish muzzle; he has very deep flews, high temples, large nostrils, and is very much underhung, and, for his size, short in the face. His eyes are tolerably full, and a good deal of the white is shown; the 'stop', or indentation between the eyes, is large and deep, and runs high up the head. The skin about the head is very loose, and falls into wrinkles and folds when the ears of the dog are erected; and a deep double dewlap runs from the angles of the mouth to the sternum. His ears have been cut out, very little of the burr being left, and this greatly detracts from the apparent size of the head. His neck is arched, short, very thick and muscular, and covered with quantities of loose skin; the shoulders broad and flat at the top, standing well out from the ribs; the forearm very thick, and slightly bowed; feet large and round, and furnished with very strong claws; the chest is great, and not only broad, but deep, and the ribs are very round. There is a considerable fall at the shoulders, and from that point the loins begin to rise, the arch terminating at the insertion of the tail. This is placed very low, has a downward crook at the root and another at the end, is very short and fine in bone, and is never erected so high as the level of the dog's back. The loins are strong and muscular, as are the hind-quarters, the stifles turning out slightly, and the hocks rather close together. The whole of the hind-quarters are small, as compared with the fore-quarters, and are considerably higher. The coat is very fine and smooth, and the hair very hard in texture. In showing condition Toro weighs 90lb. The following are his exact measurements: Head twenty-two ins; chop, close up to the eye, fourteen ins; length of face from corner of eye to tip of nose, two and a half ins; from corner of eye down to angle of mouth five ins; between eyes two and three quarter ins; from ear to ear across forehead, five and a half ins; from top of nose to under-jaw, three ins; projection of lower incisors beyond those in the upper-jaw when the mouth is closed, one ins; between canines in upper-jaw, two and a quarter ins lower-jaw, about two ins (being broken); round neck, nineteen ins; length of neck, five ins; round ribs, thirty-one ins; across chest, thirteen ins; between forelegs, nine ins; length of neck and body from apex of skull to root of tail, thirty ins; round forearm, eight and a half ins; round loins, twenty-one ins; height at shoulder, twenty-two ins; from point of elbow to ground, eleven ins.

"Toro, although very forbidding in appearance, is exceedingly quiet and docile, and is possessed of great intelligence; he retains all the peculiar attributes of the ancient British Bulldog – such as size, courage, etc. He will only pin an animal by the head, and when fighting is perfectly silent and utterly regardless of pain. He is rather slow in his movements, has a rolling kind of gait, and carries his head low."

It is believed that this dog may have been the product of a mating between a type of Spanish Mastiff and Bulldogs previously exported from England to the continent. Dogs of this type were referred to as "Spanish milk-cart dogs".

THE FORMATION OF A BREED CLUB

With this new, but very real threat of cross-breeding the pure Bulldog lines which remained, several fanciers decided that the interests of the breed could be best protected by the formation of a breed club.

In 1864 a club was formed by Mr R. S. Rockstro, an admirer of the breed, and at the inaugural meeting on November 3rd that year Mr Rockstro was made Honorary Secretary. The club was to be called 'The Bulldog Club' and its main objective would be: "the perpetuation and the improvement of the Old English Bulldog". The club's motto was decided upon as "Hold Fast", but unfortunately this was not to be – the club lasted for just three years.

Although this club's achievements were not great, one accomplishment it is credited with is the writing of the first Bulldog breed standard or, as it was known at the time, "The Properties of a Perfect Bulldog". This standard was referred to as the "Philo-Kuon" which was, in fact, the nom de plume of Samuel Wickens who drew up this manuscript and published it in February 1865. There are many similarities between this and the standard of our present-day Bulldog Club (Inc.), which was drawn up some ten years later, in 1875.

THE PHILO-KUON STANDARD OF THE BRITISH BULLDOG (Canis Pugnax)

The British Bulldog is a majestic, ancient animal, very scarce, much maligned, and as a rule, very little understood. If treated with kindness, often noticed and frequently with his master, he is a quiet and tractable dog: but if kept chained up and little noticed, he becomes less sociable and docile and, if excited and made savage, he is a most dangerous animal. He is generally an excellent guard, an extraordinary water dog, and very valuable to cross with Terriers, Pointers, Hounds, Greyhounds, etc., to give them courage and endurance. He is the boldest and most resolute of animals. The Gamecock is a courageous bird, but he will only attack his own species; but there is nothing a good Bulldog will not attack, and ever brave and unappalled, with matchless courage, he will give up only with life itself. This noble dog becomes degenerate abroad – in truth he is a national animal and is perfectly identified with Old England, and he is a dog of which Englishman may be proud.

Properties

1. The head should be large and high, that is, with elevation about the temples, and deeply sunken between the eyes, which indentation is termed 'The Stop'. This 'Stop' should extend some distance up the head. The skin of the head should be wrinkled, and the cheeks should extend outwards well beyond the eyes. The forehead of the dog should not be prominent as in the King Charles Spaniel, and not be too round, or it would be 'Apple Headed'. The head of a fine dog, fifty pounds in weight, should measure round the thickest part about twenty inches.

2. The Eyes should be wide apart, almost black, of moderate size, rather full than otherwise, round, and not deeply set. The line of the eyes should be at right-angles with the line of the face, and the eyes placed quite in front of the head, as far from the ear and as near the nose as possible.

3. The Ears should be small, thin, and wide apart. They should be either 'Rose', 'Button' or 'Tulip'. The 'Rose' ear falls backward, while the ends lap over outwards, exposing part of the inside. The 'Button' ear differs from the 'Rose' only in falling over forwards, which hides the interior. The 'Tulip' ear is nearly erect. These are the only distinct sorts of ear, but there are various grades between them, and sometimes one almost merges into the other, for the dog does not always carry them in the same manner; as for instance, the ear which is naturally a 'Rose' ear may become almost a 'Tulip' ear when the animal is excited.

4. The Nostrils should be wide, and the nose large and almost between the eyes, and black and deep; thus taking the depth of the nose, and the length from the eye to the end of the nose, the distance ought to be about the same. There should be a well-defined line straight up between the nostrils. The best bred dogs will be liable to flesh or spotted noses; this is a blemish, but no sign of bad breeding; true bred Bulldogs will occasionally have flesh coloured noses.

5. The Muzzle should be broad, deep, and short, with the skin deeply wrinkled, and underhung, but not showing the teeth; for if the mouth be even they are termed 'Shark-headed', which is considered a very bad point. The under-jaw should be square, and well up-turned, with plenty of space in a nearly straight line for the six small front teeth in the lower jaw between the tusks. This is an important point, because it denotes width and squareness of under-jaw.

6. The Neck should be moderate in length, thick, and arched at the back, with plenty of loose wrinkled skin about the throat. The Ribs should be well-rounded, and the Chest wide, deep, and rounded. The Tail should be inserted rather low down; thick where it joins the

body, long and thin, and turned round at the end, in which case it is termed a 'Ring' or 'Tiger' tail, similar to that of the Greyhound, but shorter. The perfect tail is shown in the print of Mr. Lovell's 'Ball', and the tail nearest approaching that is the nearest to perfection. 'The tail thin and taper, curling over the back or hanging down, termed Tiger-tailed; rarely erected except when the passions of the animal are aroused,' vide 'Cynographia Britannica', A.D.1800.

7. The Back should be short and arched in the loins, termed 'Roach-backed', wide across the shoulders and narrow across the loins. The Roach-back is shown in perfection in the print of 'Crib and Rosa'. Rosa's shape is perfect.

8. The Legs. The forelegs should be stout, with well-marked calves, bowed outwards, short and very wide apart. The hind legs should be slightly longer in proportion than the forelegs, so as to elevate the loins. The hocks should approach each other, which involves the stifles being turned outwards, and well-rounded, which seems to obstruct the dog's speed in running, but is admirably adapted to progressive motion when combatting on his belly. The Feet should be moderately round; not so round as a Cat's nor so long as a Hare's feet, and should be well split-up between the toes. The forefeet should be straight, and should show the knuckles well. The pasterns should be strong, that the dog may walk well on his toes.

9. The Coat should be fine, short and close. The Bulldog has a very peculiar carriage, heavy and rather slow. He rolls very much in his gait, and generally runs rather sideways; his hind legs are seldom lifted very high, so that his hind feet (which, like the stifles are turned outwards), appear to skim the ground.

10. The Colour should be salmon, fallow, red, brindled, or white with these colours variously pied. The salmon and fallow with black muzzles, called 'Smuts', are choice colours. Some greatly admire the white, but a bright salmon with black muzzle would be the choicest of all colours. Black was formerly considered a good colour, but black-and-tan, and blue, are very bad colours. There is a strong resemblance between a brindled Bulldog and a striped Hyena.

11. Weight. A Bulldog seldom weighs more than sixty pounds. If larger he may be suspected of the Mastiff cross. On the other hand, he ought not to be less than twenty pounds in weight or he may be suspected of being crossed with the Terrier. The large Bulldogs are grander and more striking in their proportions than the small ones.

London, February, 1865.   Philo-Kuon.

DOG EXHIBITIONS

Not surprisingly the exhibiting of dogs became a popular pastime and when the Bulldog "King Dick" was exhibited at the Birmingham show in 1861 he caused much interest, and is now regarded by many as the forerunner of the type seen today. He was bred by Mr J. Lamphier and it was said that King Dick's strain could be traced back over a hundred years. He was a red smut and weighed forty-eight pounds. He swept the board at all of the important shows for many years.

Around the end of the century the breed was still divided by weight, being classified as over eighteen pounds and under eighteen pounds with the classes for the miniature bulldogs

A painting by Arthur Wardle 1924. Top row: Pen-y-lan Duchess, and Hefty Son-o-Mike. Bottom row: Tufnell Launtett, Milgrange Marquis, Failsworth White Orry and Bucccaneer.

The famous Ch. Pugilist, owned by Mrs B. J. Waltz, winner of thirty Challenge Certificates during the 1930s.

usually well filled. It is widely believed that these 'Toy' Bulldogs, some of whom were exported to France, became the forerunners of the French Bulldog seen today.

Another exhibit considered outstanding around this time was 'Crib', again the property of Mr Lamphier. Crib, a brindle and white, was a heavyweight at sixty-four pounds but extraordinarily active. One of the best judges of the day considered Crib to possess 'as near 100% of show points as could possibly be found in a single dog'.

Classes were scheduled for the breed at the earliest dog shows held in the UK. In fact by the time the most famous of dog shows, Crufts, came into being in 1891, Bulldogs had already been exhibited for thirty years, and the first winners of the dog and bitch Crufts challenge classes were the fifty-first and fifty-second Bulldog champions to gain their titles. These were the dog Ch. Bedgebury Lion, owned and bred by Mr P. Beresford-Hope, and the

*'Everybody's
Loved by
Someone'*

*'Love's Golden
Dream has
Passed'*

*These photographic studies, taken in the 1930s, epitomise
the Bulldog's unique place in British affections.*

bitch Ch. Dryad, owned by Sam Woodiwiss and bred by Mr G.J.Padbury. The only Bulldog ever to win Best in Show at Crufts was Ch. Noways Chuckles in 1952. Chuckles was owned and bred by John and Marjorie Barnard.

THE BULLDOG CLUB

In April 1875 the club which still remains the premier UK Bulldog breed club today, and in fact is the oldest breed club in the world, 'The Bulldog Club Incorporated', was founded. One of this club's main objectives was to combat the menace of attempts to introduce the blood of the Spanish milk-cart dog (Spanish Bulldog) by which means it was sought to increase the weight of the breed to between one hundred and one hundred and twenty pounds. A remarkable feature of this club is that its first annual subscription of one guinea (£1.05) has remained unchanged to the present day.

Among its many achievements was the drawing up of the breed standard which is still in use today and is constantly used for reference by fanciers the world over. It was published in *The Country* on May 27th 1875. Although the UK Kennel Club standard varies slightly, it is still basically the same as this document drawn up well over a century ago, and Bulldoggers worldwide are very proud of this fact.

The first annual show held under the auspices of the club took place at the Alexandra Palace on June 14th and 15th 1875. The chief prize went to Mr Turton's Crib, bred by Mr Lamphier. By the end of the eighteen-hundreds the Bulldog had made his mark in the show ring not only in the United Kingdom but throughout the world.

Ch. Kingrock Canis Pugnax: Owned and bred by Chris Thomas.
The Bulldog has a strong character, but the breed's phlegmatic approach to life makes it an
ideal companion.
Pearce.

Chapter Three

CHOOSING A BULLDOG

CHARACTER

The Bulldog's strength of character is one of the breed's greatest attributes. The dogs have an unruffled attitude to life, combined with an ability to adapt to just about any situation with an almost phlegmatic approach, which makes them ideal companions to have about the house for those dog owners who have little patience with the more highly strung breeds.

This is not to say that there is any lack of ability to guard – far from it – but a Bulldog will do just what is necessary to protect the things that really matter, namely family and home: nothing more and nothing less.

Although the Bulldog could not be considered to be among the most biddable of breeds, it is often this very characteristic which appeals to Bulldog devotees. They are not dogs blindly to obey your every command, but will give each request from the owner careful consideration before coming to a decision on whether or not to obey. If you believe a dog should jump on command, then a Bulldog is certainly not for you, as a battle of wills is not a good idea with this rather stubborn breed.

LIVING WITH OTHER ANIMALS

I am often asked how a Bulldog will respond to other four-legged members of the family, be they canine, feline or whatever. In my experience Bulldogs will accept the companionship of virtually any animal, provided they are introduced in an appropriate manner and while as young as possible.

It is of course most important to avoid unnecessary confrontation between the newcomer and those already established within a household and, to a great extent, this can be avoided by following one or two common sense precautions; for example picking up toys and bones, which if left can so easily cause conflict. It is also not a good idea to feed your latest acquisition in the general area that has been the feeding place of established residents and, certainly in the early days, it is better whenever possible to feed in separate rooms.

It seems that, however many beds there are available, there is a communal preference for one, although this seldom causes a problem as either all of the dogs end up sharing a bed, or the more dominant dog will choose the best place and the rest will have to make do with

Fin. Est. Ch. Tretun Bustersam of Kingrock: Top winning Bulldog in Finland in 1991, and 1992. Top stud 1993. Bulldogs make excellent family dogs, and are well-known for getting on with children.

what is left. Cats are not normally a problem to introduce to Bulldogs. I have always had a number of cats around the kennels, as I believe if the dogs are brought up seeing cats on a regular basis from puppyhood, they are less likely to take any notice if there is a cat in residence in their new home.

Introducing a puppy to other pets is generally much easier than bringing in an adult dog, but that is not to say that the latter cannot be done. Many Bulldogs, who have, sadly, needed rehoming through the Bulldog rescue service, have happily adapted to living amongst other animals for the first time in their lives.

MAKING THE FIRST DECISIONS

Before going to view a litter of puppies, there are one or two elements to take into account. It is all too easy, particularly if it is the very first time you have seen a litter of puppies, to forget all of the carefully discussed plans and to end up falling for the appealing puppy sitting in the corner just asking to be taken home. The question is: is this the right puppy for you?

One of the first considerations must be that of gender. I am constantly surprised at the number of people who telephone our kennel enquiring about the availability of puppies, who have given little or no thought to this matter, although one will often find that other less important considerations, such as colour, have been discussed in detail.

Generally speaking, over the years the demand for dog and bitch puppies has been pretty equally balanced, with perhaps slightly more demand for bitches. I feel that we in Bulldogs are fortunate in this as it is the very appearance of the Bulldog male, being more impressive than that of the female, which is instrumental in helping to ensure that the demand from the general public for dog puppies as pets will always be there.

The decision is ultimately one of personal choice and the temperament and strength of character of either sex is legendary, and unlike that of any other breed. The Bulldog's docile nature and suitability as a companion to children is universally acknowledged.

COPING WITH A BITCH

Before deciding on a bitch puppy there are one or two points which should be given consideration. Decide whether you have any intention of breeding from your Bulldog at a later date. This is a difficult breed and generally considered unsuitable for those with little experience of dog breeding. Remember that the welfare of a bitch in whelp is, to a great extent, in your hands and, although the services of a veterinary surgeon will probably be required at some stage, decisions will need to be made which may leave the inexperienced breeder feeling somewhat out of his or her depth. Remember also that if you do decide to breed from your bitch, the responsiblity of finding suitable homes for the resultant puppies will rest squarely on your shoulders.

Then there is the consideration of coping with a bitch during her season. Although there is no predictable time lapse between seasons, as a rule most Bulldog bitches come in season at six monthly intervals. Most will show a fairly heavy discharge (usually referred to as 'colour' in doggy circles) during the early stages of the season and some for the full twenty-one days. Because of the rather stocky build of this breed, most bitches find it difficult to keep themselves clean in this area and consequently you must be prepared to cover her favourite chair (if she is allowed on the furniture), light-coloured carpets, and anything else which she is likely to come in contact with and is not easily washable.

For this reason some owners prefer to keep their bitches confined to one room of the house, the kitchen for instance, during this time – but it does seem somewhat unfair to confine an animal which would normally have the run of the house.

As most vets are not keen on spaying bitches, unless on medical grounds, the drawbacks of the seasonal cycle, although not a major problem, should be considered before finally deciding on the purchase of a bitch puppy.

Having visited the homes of many breeders over the years I have been surprised to find that a fairly large number of them actually started in the breed by purchasing a male as a pet, with no intention of showing and breeding. However, it is often the case that, once the Bulldog bug has truly bitten and interest in the breed becomes more than just that of the pet owner, it becomes apparent that perhaps the purchasing of a male was not such a good idea after all. Although much fun may be had in the show ring with a Bulldog male, if you wish to become more seriously involved in the breed, especially in creating your own line, a bitch puppy will be a better foundation animal, as a dog in the hands of a beginner is most unlikely to attract stud work.

ESTABLISHING A LINE

There is usually a good demand for well-bred stock from those wishing to establish their own line in the breed and are consequently on the look-out for a good foundation bitch.

Particularly if you are interested in showing or breeding, it is far better to buy from an established breeder, for, although newcomers to the breed producing their first litter may be full of good intentions and do all they can to advise prospective purchasers, it is very often a case of the blind leading the blind. Over the years many puppies have been sold as having show potential but displaying faults which would have been apparent at the time of sale and are often not noticed by inexperienced breeders.

Of course even the nicest puppy can turn out to be of just pet quality, but that is no excuse for selling puppies with congenital faults such as coat or eye colour, which will prevent them winning in the show ring, as show potential. It would be far wiser for newer breeders to either explain the position to purchasers and let them select their own choice or, better still, get someone who is more experienced in the breed to look at the litter and sort out those puppies which can fairly be sold as show potential from those purely destined for the pet market.

It is worth drawing your attention to the expression 'show potential', as opposed to 'show quality' which, apart from being misleading, as no-one can predict with any degree of certainty that a puppy will be of show quality when reaching maturity, can also leave the breeder exposed to all sorts of legal problems at a later date if the puppy does not come up to expectations. Therefore, remember that an eight-to-ten week old puppy can be described as 'of show potential' but not 'of show quality'.

INSPECTING A PUPPY
It is extremely difficult to give detailed instructions as to what to look for in a puppy, as different lines tend to develop at varying speeds and what may be considered over-done in one line may be considered to be quite acceptable at that stage in another.

Generally speaking you are looking for a well-balanced puppy with good bone and square front. The head should have sufficient work (wrinkle) but not to an excessive extent, with plenty of loose skin over the entire body and particularly around the neck, forming a dewlap.

The skin should be free of blemishes and clean, with no sign of a rash or other skin irritation. The eyes should be clear and bright, with no sign of discharge, and dark in colour.

The tail should of course be straight, but few are, and this should not be considered as a major factor when deciding on a puppy. It is often the case that puppies' tails, especially if straight, will appear far too long in comparison to the rest of the body. But it is a fact that puppies DO grow into their tails, which should not be artificially shortened under any circumstances.

Another aspect of the tail is the carriage, which in many puppies will appear to be far higher than it will be in adulthood. It is quite normal to see puppies wagging their tails higher than their toplines but, providing the tail carriage is downward, the chances are that, providing neither of the parents have 'gay' tails, the puppy will ultimately have good tail carriage.

Screw tails can sometimes be extremely close fitting to the body and may create problems at a later date but, as some which appear to be quite free in young puppies seem to grow

A litter of Smasher Bulldogs, aged seven weeks, bred in the USA. It takes an expert eye to pick out a puppy with show potential.

Kingrock Captain Christian and Merriveen Maybe Baby, pictured at nine weeks of age. Sired by Merriveen Son of Satan out of Kingrock My-Nora-Tee, both of these puppies went on to become UK Champions.

Ch. Amurton Dirty Harry at Kingrock owned by Chris Thomas and Graham Godfrey, bred by Les and Sigrid Crumpton, pictured after winning the Spillers Dog World Puppy Stakes, beating 443 puppies, handled by Pat Meredith.

tighter to the body with maturity, it is one of those things which you will have to cope with when the time comes, and it would be a big mistake to reject an otherwise nice puppy purely because of a screw tail. Remember that most champions have screw tails.

Ears can be a problem in as much as some puppies will still have the ear carriage known as the 'button' ear, at the time of sale. This ear carriage, similar to that of the Boxer, was seen as acceptable in the first breed standard (the Philo-Kuon), along with the tulip ear (almost erect) and the rose ear. However in the first official standard of the Bulldog Club Incorporated (1875) the only ear carriage considered as correct was that of the rose ear that we see today.

If the ears are showing signs of rosing back naturally, all well and good, but if at ten to twelve weeks they are still in the button position, the help of an experienced breeder will have to be called upon to stick the ear in position – usually with the use of a rubber-based glue which does not damage the ear but just holds it in the correct position for long enough to allow the muscles to set in the desired position.

Whether set artificially or not, it is a good policy not to play around with a Bulldog puppy's ears as they are quite delicate and the carriage can be spoilt for life. Once the dog has reached maturity the ear carriage is set and only serious damage will alter the shape.

If you are buying a dog-puppy for show, remember to check that he has both of his testicles descended into the scrotum.

Chapter Four

CARING FOR YOUR PUPPY

Before your puppy arrives home there are a few things you must have sorted out, to save you having problems later on.

SLEEPING QUARTERS
Where is the puppy to sleep, and in what sort of bed? The oval plastic dog beds are very suitable for young puppies as they are easily cleaned, draught-proof and quite difficult (although not impossible) to destroy. Whatever type of bed you have decided upon, it is better to get your puppy used to sleeping in it right from the start. It is most unfair to expect a youngster to accept being moved around the house – and the idea of taking the puppy up to your bed for just the first day or so is definitely a big mistake.

A puppy needs lots of reassurance when it first arrives in its new home.

If you have decided on the kitchen, for example, as your puppy's bedroom, when bed-time comes you must ensure that it contains a warm bed with a familiar blanket, a toy or two to play with if the puppy should wake in the night, and a bowl of water. Make sure that the baby Bulldog has recently eaten, as puppies tend to settle far more quickly on a full tummy. Remember also to put newspaper down for use during the night.

Although it may not be easy, if the puppy cries in the night do not respond. Unless the puppy is cold, in which case some form of additional heating will need to be found, there really is no need. Puppies are very quick to learn that, if they wake in the night and want a little human company, a couple of pitiful yelps will usually bring one running. Bulldog puppies are usually very quick to settle in their new home and, if you can avoid the temptation to go down for the first couple of nights, they will soon start to go through the night silently.

FEEDING

There are as many different ways to feed a puppy as there are dog breeders. Some prefer to keep to the tried and tested feeding regimes with which they have had success for many years. On the other hand there are those, myself included, who prefer to trust modern technology to come up with a more balanced diet than would be possible using the old techniques.

It is a fact that complete foods have improved out of all recognition in recent years and many breeders, who at one time would not have entertained the notion of feeding their young stock in such a way, are now using this method of feeding almost exclusively.

The problem with changing over to a complete food often seems to be more a psychological one for the breeder than a practical one, and the concept that puppies do not need a diet of fresh meat and biscuit to thrive can be hard for some dog breeders of the old school to accept.

This does not mean to say that all complete foods, even those developed specifically for puppies, are going to supply an adequate source of nutrition. As with everything, it is very much a case of 'getting what you pay for' and it is money well spent to purchase one of the more expensive 'expanded' foods. To economise at this crucial stage of a dog's development would be a false economy indeed.

It is unnecessary to vary a puppy's food with each meal but, unfortunately for the pet food manufacturers, it is a fact that puppies quickly become bored with the same basic diet at each feed. For this reason I explain to new owners that, although the complete food contains an adequately balanced diet, including the correct amounts of vitamins and minerals, if your puppy does not eat a sufficient amount of food, body weight will be lost very quickly and this is something which should be avoided at all costs.

Generally speaking, all that is needed to encourage your puppy to eat the required amount of complete food, is to mix with it a very small quantity of something tasty, for example canned dog food mixed with warm water and then stirred into the meal, or a little meat gravy or even some table scraps.

I always soak complete foods in warm water for some hours before feeding and this is particularly important with the expanded foods.

Your puppy will probably come to you aged between eight to ten weeks, so should be fully weaned and have no problem taking food from a bowl. I have found that a small, shallow plastic bowl, about the diameter of a tea plate, is sufficient for the first few weeks.

By the time our puppies are ready to go to new homes they are having a diet virtually free of dairy produce. Milk feeds are stopped by the time our puppies are two months of age. A small quantity of milk is added to the morning feed as an appetiser but, if this has the effect of making the puppies' motions loose, it is stopped immediately. It is most important to make sure that an adequate supply of fresh drinking water is available at all times, and we have found the heavy stone dog bowls to be the most satisfactory for, although some Bulldogs will insist on trying to dig the water out, few will actually bother to try to pick up a heavy dish.

At eight weeks of age our puppies would be having five meals a day, but by the age of ten weeks this is reduced to four. They are kept on this regime for some time and, at around four months, cut down to three meals a day. By the age of six to seven months, they are normally being fed twice daily, and some owners prefer to keep to this throughout the dog's life. I have found this to be preferable, but many owners do feed just once a day, giving a biscuit snack at bed time.

HOUSE TRAINING

It is certainly not a good idea to allow your puppy to wander around the house unsupervised. Remember that a puppy needing to spend a penny will do it often without warning and is no respecter of carpets, Persian or otherwise. Also take into account that when those teething pains begin, anything which may relieve the pain by means of a quick chew will be considered fair game. For these reasons the kitchen is usually considered to be the room most suited to the requirements of a puppy.

The chances are that your puppy will already be paper-trained but most unlikely to be able to go through the night without the need of this facility for some weeks. The kitchen's durable floor surface can be ideal as it can cope with any accidents. Do not forget to praise the pup when the paper is used, although with the disorientation of a new home, it may take a day or two before full paper training is achieved. Usually puppies want to relieve themselves following a meal and on first waking, so when you see the tell-tale sign of running around in circles, lift the puppy on to the paper and give lots of praise afterwards.

If you have your new arrival during the summer months there is no reason why the puppy should not be allowed out into the garden for a short time. If you have designated a particular part of it which you would like the puppy to use, then, when the puppy shows the unmistakable signs of needing to relieve itself, take the puppy there, get a satisfactory result and, again, make a big fuss afterwards.

House training is of course easier during the nice weather but, with a little perseverance, it should not be long before the puppy begins to realise that going in the ordained area brings plenty of praise, although Bulldog puppies are notorious for suddenly having little lapses, during which time they revert to their pre-house-trained days. This is usually just a stage that they are going through and it is unusual to find adult Bulldogs that are not house trained – although they do expect someone to be around when they need to go out.

HEALTH

Inoculations should be started at around eight to nine weeks of age. Most vets prefer not to give the second inoculation until the puppy is at least twelve weeks old and, regardless of the age at which the course is started, the inoculations should be at least two weeks apart. There will then be a further delay of two weeks before it will be safe to take your puppy out into the wide world.

Keeping your puppy free from worms is very important and you should ask the breeder when your puppy was last wormed and with what. You can then pass this information on to your vet, who will advise you as to a suitable vermifuge and give you instructions as to when and how. These days, worming a puppy is extremely simple, usually involving little more than mixing some powder or a crushed tablet with your puppy's food.

TEETHING AND TOYS

Bearing in mind that your puppy will soon start teething, it is a good idea to have a variety of toys available from the outset. Rubber toys are ideal provided that they are too big for the puppy to swallow. Keep an eye on them and when they begin to break up and pieces of rubber are starting to come away, it is safer to dispose of them. Beef-hide chews are not safe for Bulldogs as they chew them until they have reverted to a piece of slippery hide, and will then often attempt to swallow them whole, as the novelty of chewing has by this stage worn off. Several Bulldogs have been known to choke in this way. Nylon toys are ideal as they are practically indestructible; sterilised marrow bones can provide hours of fun safely. Biscuit bones are also a handy treat to have around the house and most Bulldogs love them.

PORTABLE CRATES

One really useful piece of equipment is a collapsible wire dog-crate. These started to become popular in the UK with showgoers a few years ago, and now a high percentage of exhibitors use them, not only on the show bench to ensure that their dog does not escape, but also in the back of an estate car, as it makes an ideal travelling kennel. A Bulldog accustomed from an early age to being confined to the crate for short periods, will prefer travelling in a crate rather than loose in the car, and feel far safer. Another benefit of these crates, where the new puppy is concerned, is that it gives you a portable pen which can be folded flat but is an ideal place to put your puppy at night, thus preventing any damage being done, particularly during the teething stage. For those with an estate car the crate is certainly money well spent, and they are available at most shows or through your pet shop. I use one measuring thirty inches long by twenty-one inches wide and twenty-four inches high. This size fits onto a show bench and is also large enough to contain an adult Bulldog for short periods.

BASIC OBEDIENCE TRAINING

Around the home particularly, there is the need for your bulldog to understand some basic obedience commands. The voice is all-important in this and will usually have far more effect than smacking, which should be avoided wherever possible. Do not confuse your puppy by using too many words meaning the same thing. It is hardly surprising that your

Aust. Ch. Snobul Dream Lover and Aust. Ch. Snobul Bonnie Bess. A good diet, clean sleeping quarters and regular exercise are all essential ingredients in rearing Bulldogs so that they can reach their full potential.

puppy is somewhat muddled if the command used to stop doing something varies from 'stop it' to 'don't do that' to 'pack it up'. The command 'no' is soon readily understood and should be used whenever necessary. With regard to house training, I always use the same command – 'be a clean boy' or 'be a clean girl' when the puppy has been placed on newspaper or has advanced to being taken outside and placed in the area for spending a penny. They very quickly learn that this command means to get on with what it is that they have been taken outside to do, and can be quite helpful when, due to either a shortage of time or inclement weather conditions, one does not wish to stand in the garden for ten minutes while puppy explores the area.

Basic obedience is simply a case of showing right from wrong and what is considered acceptable from what is not. This applies to such things as whether your puppy is allowed onto the furniture or allowed to go upstairs. In these cases just a firm 'no' and lifting away from the immediate area is generally all that is required.

LEAD TRAINING

Bulldogs have an inbuilt reluctance to be led anywhere and, for this reason, the earlier one can start to lead train, within reason, the better. We have found the light nylon show leads to be ideal and, as we do not leave collars on our dogs, the collar and lead all-in-one works very well. The type I prefer does not choke; it has a clip which slides down, stopping the collar from coming back over the puppy's head, but it does not tighten if pulled on. This is most important, as frightening a puppy during the first experiences on the lead will make training far more difficult. Although the puppy may not be old enough to go out, due to incomplete inoculations or whatever, it is still a good idea to get the puppy used to walking around the house and garden with a lead on and this can be done for just a few minutes a day from approximately seven weeks of age.

Incidentally, never allow your Bulldogs off the lead when away from home. No matter how much you may think you have everything under control, Bulldogs are incredibly obstinate and, if they see something in the distance that they want to explore, not only can they find from somewhere an incredible turn of speed but will often suffer temporary deafness as you scream fruitlessly for their return – which not only gives amusement to those around but is extremely dangerous if there are busy roads in the area. Remember, when you are finally reunited, it is most unfair to chastise your dog, as it was your fault for removing the lead and the stubbornness is a characteristic of the breed and should be accepted as such.

Most Bulldogs greatly enjoy travelling in the car and it is a good idea to take them for short journeys from an early age. As we always travel our dogs in purpose-made wire crates suitable for use in an estate car, puppies have to accept this from the very beginning and they quickly get used to being in the back of the car. This will not be the case if you first allow your puppy to travel on a seat and then, at a later date, decide that the rear of the vehicle should be used as the travelling place. The same basic rule applies to car training as to any other training during those crucial first few weeks – 'start off as you mean to go on', for these early lessons will form the habits of a life time.

Chapter Five

ADULT MAINTENANCE

HOUSING

Bulldogs thrive as house pets as they love the company of the family around them. Unfortunately it is not always possible to keep them in this way if you start to acquire more, either through breeding and keeping a promising youngster, or buying in more stock. The time will soon come when accommodation outside of the home will have to be considered.

To keep Bulldogs in kennels is not so much unkind as, perhaps, a little unfortunate, as the Bulldog's true character cannot show itself to full potential in a kennel environment. The Bulldog is a breed which thrives on companionship and it will be necessary to spend as much time as possible with kennel dogs in order to compensate for the lack of a home environment.

Generally we try to kennel our Bulldogs in pairs, as they certainly seem to appreciate the company of another Bulldog, but this is not always possible and certain animals will show a definite preference towards living on their own. Over the years we have been able to keep the majority of our stud dogs kennelled with a bitch for company although, of course, a close eye must be kept on her when she is due in season, and they must be separated throughout this period.

AVOIDING FIGHTS

Bitches do seem to be at their most unsociable just prior to coming into season and, if we do have a fight between two bitches, either kennelled or house pets, the nearness of their seasons are the first thing that we check for.

In any breed of dog a fight can suddenly occur, often for no explicable reason. We take every possible precaution to try to avoid this happening, for example by feeding dogs which share a kennel well away from each other or, better still, separately, and not giving toys or biscuits when the dogs are to be left unattended – the time when most fights seem to occur.

If you can avoid trouble between kennel-mates so much the better, for Bulldogs have extremely good memories and once animosity has been allowed to develop between two dogs it is sometimes impossible ever to get them to share a kennel again. For this reason above all, prevention is better than cure.

Aust. Ch. Nonparell Maggie Thatch (left) and Aust. Ch. Oushiinu Lady Bonita.
Bulldogs generally seem to enjoy each other's company.

KENNEL CONSTRUCTION

With regard to the construction of the buildings at Kingrock, we have used both wood and brick-built buildings and I must admit that, although we currently have none in use, the wooden buildings always have a warmer feel to them; but this may be purely psychological, as wood looks so much warmer than brick or concrete.

From a maintenance point of view, brick buildings are infinitely better, being easier to disinfect and to draught-proof, and are virtually indestructible, which is a major consideration, as Bulldogs in a kennel situation, where they can easily become bored, can become great chewers and demolish a wooden building in a very short space of time once they put their minds to it.

It should also be borne in mind that regulations regarding the kennelling of dogs are continually being revised and the probability is that, in the future, only kennels which can be disinfected easily, such as brick or concrete ones, will be licensed, as is currently the case with boarding kennels.

Our kennels measure five foot by five foot and are six foot six inches in height at their lowest point. Although they do not need to be this high – in the past we have managed perfectly well with kennels which measured just four foot six inches in height – it is certainly much easier from a maintenance point of view to have a kennel in which you can stand up. Also, as the only form of heat supplied to our kennel dogs is that from infra-red bulbs or 'dull emitters' hung from the roof, the added height is most useful, to avoid any danger of the dogs being able to touch the heaters.

The kennel floors are made of concrete and then covered with wood shavings, which are changed daily. The dogs are given plastic beds with blankets on which to sleep. The veterinary-type imitation sheepskin seem to be the most easy blankets to manage as they wash well and dry in a short space of time – a big consideration as all blankets are machine-washed at least every other day and sometimes every day in winter, when they quickly become dirty and damp from the dogs walking in and out from their exercise runs.

The exercise runs themselves are, again, concrete-based, with a drainage channel at one end to take away surplus water during the daily hosing down. The wall partitions between the runs are just three feet in height, which is high enough to keep the dogs contained, whilst allowing them to look over into the adjoining kennel and run, thereby gaining the impression of being less confined. Although we have had several extremely athletic Bulldogs, we have yet to have one jump over a run wall of this height.

Each run measures sixteen foot by five foot and this provides adequate space for two Bulldogs although, while their kennels are being cleaned and their runs hosed each day, the dogs are put into an exercise area to run off any surplus energy. This is also the area in which we introduce to each other dogs which are to eventually become kennel mates: it is not a good policy just to put one dog into another's kennel without this preliminary meeting.

As previously mentioned, the only form of heating supplied is in the form of infra-red heaters hung above each bed, but these are only used in extreme weather conditions and, because our kennels are situated in a part of the country where the temperature rarely falls much below freezing, they are not called upon very often. Young stock or dogs which have been used to living inside the house and may be staying for stud, for example, are of course a different matter, and some extra heat may well be required.

At the other end of the spectrum, another of the advantages of the brick-built kennel is that it tends to stay cool in the summer, and double-insulating the roof helps not only in reducing condensation in the winter but also in maintaining a cool temperature throughout hot periods.

In addition to the kennel blocks we also have puppy rooms, which are used basically for the whelping and rearing of puppies. With a breed which is as labour-intensive as the Bulldog, it is helpful to have an attractive and well-lit environment, as much time is spent with the bitch during the first few weeks after whelping. Inside the puppy room are pens made of six foot by six foot weldmesh panels, which enable the mothers to be confined but in a position to see all that is going on.

The only other building which actually forms part of our kennel is the dog kitchen, an absolute necessity if a number of dogs is being kept and also for licensing purposes. In our dog kitchen we also have a bath for the dogs, and driers; it also houses the freezers which contain the dogs' meat.

ADDITIONAL EXERCISE FOR KENNEL DOGS

Although the dogs receive adequate exercise, we do try to ensure that each one spends a little time on the lead at least every other day. Not only will this ensure that they will remain lead-trained but, more importantly, it gives the kennel dog the opportunity to spend a little time with the owner as an individual, and not just as one of many. The importance of spending as much time as possible with kennel dogs cannot be over-stated.

FEEDING

The way in which domestic dogs are fed has changed drastically over recent years, and the range and diversity of diets available to satisfy the needs of our canine companions is quite incredible. It can be a daunting task to select the most appropriate diet for a particular dog's needs and, often, the only real solution is that of trial and error, for what may well suit one dog may not suit another. For many years this was a 'tripe and biscuit' kennel and, apart from the rather unpleasant smell of the former (although the dogs loved it), I saw little reason for change. However several breeders changed their dogs over from a fresh to a dry food diet and seemed happy with the results. Personally, I was still not convinced that dogs could maintain condition on a diet which seemed rather unnatural in both appearance and consistency.

It was not until we had been approached by a leading 'complete food' manufacturer who, as part of their research 'in the field', were prepared to offer a six-month supply of their product free of charge, providing that we fed the kennel exclusively on it and kept a record of the dogs' condition and reaction, that we decided to give it a try. The particular food offered would certainly be considered a top-of-the-range product, and the dogs all took to it instantly. Although there was no immediate sign of improvement in condition, after a few weeks the coats did develop a noticeable bloom, and dogs which had a history of difficulty in keeping weight on, were looking positively plump. Very few of the dogs suffered adverse digestive problems during the change-over period – which came as something of a surprise and relief. When the trial was complete the results were most satisfactory. Although I eventually settled on a more competitively priced product from the same manufacturers, I would definitely not consider returning the kennel to a diet of just fresh meat and biscuits.

Generally speaking I have found that Bulldogs prefer the 'expanded' foods: these are usually in a pellet form with a slightly honeycomb effect, which is soaked for several hours before feeding, allowing it time to swell. This is most important when using dry food. It is also essential to make sure that cold, fresh drinking water is always available.

Whether feeding fresh meat and biscuit or complete food, give two meals a day. This not only avoids the possibility of overloading the stomach, which lessens the chances of bloat (gastric torsion), but, for the kennel dogs in particular, it gives them another high-light in an otherwise rather boring day.

Sterilised marrow bones are ideal playthings, even for the older Bulldog, and most will chew at them with great alacrity, helping to strengthen and clean teeth in the process.

EXERCISE

One question often asked is: "How far can a Bulldog walk?" – which is rather difficult to

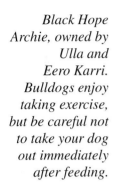

Black Hope Archie, owned by Ulla and Eero Karri. Bulldogs enjoy taking exercise, but be careful not to take your dog out immediately after feeding.

answer. Puppies should only be taken for a very short walk on their first outing – and then gradually lengthen the distance covered. As adults, most Bulldogs are content with a twenty-minute stroll each evening, but there is no reason why a Bulldog should not be capable of walking much longer distances than this, providing that they are introduced to it gradually.

It is most important to be aware of weather conditions throughout the summer months and to exercise in the early morning or in the cool of the evening. If the weather is hot or humid, do not be tempted to take your Bulldog out just because you want company. The dog would probably be much happier at home in a well-ventilated and cool room.

Do not exercise your Bulldog following a meal. As well as being uncomfortable, it can also be extremely dangerous for the dog to exercise on a full stomach.

GROOMING

The day-to-day maintenance of the Bulldog's coat must be among the simplest in the canine world. This is not to say that a cavalier approach can be taken, but if carried out routinely and correctly, few problems should arise.

Bathing a Bulldog should only be done when absolutely necessary. This is because it is the oils contained within the coat, which help repel dirt, that are washed away with the shampoo, and after each bath the coat will be left drier and less able to repel dirt and grime unassisted.

For the show ring a dog should be presented in immaculate condition, and to show a white Bulldog in pristine condition without bathing for each show is extremely difficult, as they do have a tendency to look slightly grey, no matter how clean one may try to keep them. If the need to bath should occur, it is probably as well, especially in warm weather, to use an insecticidal shampoo, available either from your vet or your pet shop. Whatever type of shampoo you decide upon, always make sure that it is specially formulated for use on dogs, as others may contain ingredients liable to cause allergic reactions.

White dogs are generally the exception though, and coloured dogs are kept in better condition by regular grooming to remove any dust and dirt, and then finishing off with a chammy leather or horse-hair brush, to obtain that lovely bloom which looks so attractive, especially on the brindles, and which is obtained by good diet, clean conditions and plenty of grooming – not out of a bottle of shampoo.

CHECKING THE SKIN

As part of a regular routine, each of our dogs is groomed with a pure bristle brush or rubber grooming-glove. The latter are available from good pet shops and are most useful for removing dead coat. The dogs are checked over for skin problems on a weekly basis. If carried out correctly, this will become an event which the dogs will look forward to, and they enjoy having that little bit of individual attention, which is particularly important in a large kennel. This weekly session gives an opportunity to check for wet creases, especially the over-nose wrinkle which, in the adult Bulldog, can get quite heavy and become damp and infected very quickly. To avoid this happening, use talcum powder suitable for use on babies rather than the scented type, and carefully apply it under any heavy wrinkles, avoiding getting powder in the eyes. It is also a good idea to powder under the tail at the same time, as, especially with a screw tail, this area can become damp and infected if not properly attended to. It is not difficult to avoid problems, but if they are once allowed to develop, they can be most difficult to cure.

If for some reason the problem has not been spotted in time and an area has become wet and infected, it is better to wash it very gently in a mild antiseptic solution and then apply an antibiotic powder dressing, which is only available through your veterinary surgeon. Using talcum power at this stage will only aggravate the problem. Remember that the use of powder in the coat of show dogs is banned by the English Kennel Club, and judges are at liberty to report any exhibit they find with traces of powder in the coat.

NOSES

Nose leathers can become dry, especially during the summer months. This can be prevented by putting a dab of vaseline on the nose each week and gently rubbing it in.

EARS

Bulldog ears usually require little attention, as the type of ear called for in the standard – the rose ear – actually permits adequate air to circulate thus avoiding the ear problems associated with certain other breeds. It is still necessary, however, to keep a look-out for any sign of dirt within the ear and, although it is not advisable to put anything deep into the ear, it will do no harm to wipe out any obvious dirt or wax with a piece of cotton wool. It is now possible to buy an ear-cleaning solution which will help remove a build-up of wax, making ear cleaning a lot easier. This again is best purchased through your vet.

TEETH

Teeth should be checked on a fairly regular basis, especially during the teething period, around five or six months of age, to ensure that the milk teeth are coming away freely and are not interfering with the progress of the adult ones. Special attention should be given to the teeth of the older Bulldog, keeping a close look-out for decay and possible signs of heavy plaque build-up, which, if necessary, can be removed by descaling the teeth.

NAILS

Nails will generally need little attention if regular exercise on a hard surface is available, but for those dogs who spend much of their time in the house or on grass in the garden it will be necessary to keep the nails trimmed. We have found it helps in later life to get puppies accustomed to having their nails trimmed regularly from just a few weeks of age. Even if the nails are not really in need of attention, still go through the procedure of taking a tiny amount off each one, just to keep the dogs accustomed to having their feet dealt with. There is nothing more daunting than having to trim the nail of an adult Bulldog who has decided to the contrary. Some breeders prefer to keep their dogs' nails filed, but I have not found this to be a suitable way of keeping them in check. Remember that Bulldogs have their dewclaws left on and, as these have no contact with the floor, they will need regular attention.

Chapter Six

HEALTH MATTERS

The Bulldog is by no means as unhealthy as some would have us believe, and it is sad when one hears of Bulldogs being decried, very often by those with little or no practical experience of the breed. This is not to say that the breed is free of problems but, taken overall, it has no more than many others.

PROBLEMS AROUND THE TAIL

Dogs with blocked anal glands will attempt to relieve the pain either by scooting along on their bottoms or sitting on their haunches and attempting to swivel around on their tails. Although this can also be an indication of a worm infestation, in most breeds the first thing to check for would be blocked anal glands. But this is not the most common reason for Bulldogs to behave in this manner, and more often than not the problem will be found around the base of the tail. Bulldogs with screw tails are especially prone to problems under the tail, especially in hot weather, though they can occur at any time of the year. Even those with straight tails will sometimes have trouble at its base where it meets the body, as this area can become hot and damp. The way to prevent this is to keep the area under the tail dry by applying a little medicated powder, during regular grooming sessions, once or twice a week. If the area is allowed to become damp and an infection becomes established, it will be necessary to pay a visit to your vet, who will be able to give you a suitable preparation to clear the problem. A tight screw tail can cause a recurring problem, and it may be necessary to have the tail removed, but this is only carried out as a last resort and is rarely necessary.

If after close inspection the tail is found to be clean and dry underneath and the dog is still showing signs of distress, the best course of action would be to consult your vet, who will be able to tell whether or not the anal glands are to blame, and will empty them if necessary.

HEAT STROKE

This must be one of the biggest causes of concern to all owners of brachycephalic (short-faced) breeds, as the restricted airways, caused by the shortening of the muzzle, do make it more difficult for the dog to disperse body heat naturally, and care must be taken in certain situations not to exacerbate the situation. The strange thing about heat stroke and Bulldogs

Pride of Pencisely (Diva) with owner Wendy Howlett of Saskatoon, Saskatchewan, Canada. The Bulldog can be a surprisingly agile dog – although much depends on keeping your dog fit and healthy.

Diva negotiating the see-saw. This bitch was bred in Wales by Terry O'Donnell and exported to Canada by Chris Thomas .

is that it is not always climatic heat which is the major contributory factor. Most Bulldogs are lovers of heat and will lie out in the full sun at any opportunity.

Dogs lose body heat in a variety of ways but mainly through panting. A certain amount of heat is lost through the less coated areas of the body, the stomach for example, and as dogs only sweat through their pads, not all over as do humans, the main way of reducing heat is through respiration.

We have owned several Bulldogs who would tolerate hot weather conditions with little or no ill affect, only to display signs of heat stroke on a visit to the vet's on a moderately warm day, and it is often a mental state which will trigger off this life-threatening situation.

Although it is quite natural for a Bulldog to pant in order to lose heat, it is when this panting begins to get out of hand and brings with it the characteristic 'roaring', as it is known within the breed, that drastic action needs to be taken. Often this problem will arise

Diva going through the tyre. She is a daughter of Ch. Amurton Dirty Harry at Kingrock, who was well-known for his exuberant personality.

when away from home, and it is very much a case of 'be prepared'. Most showgoers have a routine, which is carried out right through the summer months, regarding extras that need to be carried when travelling in hot weather.

Always put a large container of water in the freezer the day before a show, and although it is not frozen solid the next day, it will contain enough ice to remain cold for most of the show day. This will give you an adequate supply of cold fresh drinking water for your dog while at the show, and plenty left over for emergencies.

If you do have a problem whilst travelling or when away from home, remember – the most important thing is to lower the dog's temperature as quickly as possible. The easiest way to do this is to pour cold water over your Bulldog, especially around the head and neck; the blood going to the brain must be cooled as quickly as possible, to prevent brain damage. This is where your container of cold water is invaluable, but if you are caught unprepared you have little time to spare and another form of cooling must be found. If there is a stream or river nearby the dog can either be stood in the shallows or water can be taken and poured over the dog. If not, find a house nearby where you can ask for access to a hosepipe. This is an ideal way of cooling a dog, as the time needed to fully reduce the heat can be quite considerable.

Another option is to find a shop which sells frozen foods. Buy a couple of packets of frozen peas or similar, as these make good temporary ice packs, but will only be of limited help. Hold these packs on the dog's head and sides of the neck. Although the dog may drink a little while being cooled, it is better not to offer too much to drink until the temperature is almost back to normal, otherwise the dog may vomit and choke.

One effective way of travelling a dog in hot weather, especially in the wire crates used at shows, is to let the dog lie on towels, soaked in cold water; but remember that it is not a good idea to cover the dog with wet towels, as this just serves to keep the heat in.

Always be aware that most tragedies that happen in hot weather are avoidable and, by taking one or two common-sense precautions, they can be prevented.

PARA-INFLUENZA

This is more commonly known as Kennel Cough, and it can be a troublesome problem, especially among the show fraternity who are constantly at risk of bringing the infection home with them from a show. Although not usually too much to worry about with strong, healthy young stock, it can be fatal to baby puppies and old dogs. The way this virus manifests itself varies considerably, from showing a slight reluctance to eat and maybe the occasional slight cough, to the hacking cough which often causes retching and even vomiting, sometimes sounding as though the dog has something stuck in its throat. Most modern inoculations contain a para-influenza vaccine, along with those for Distemper, Parvovirus, Canine Virus Hepatitis and Leptospirosis, all of which should of course be given. Some are sold separately; it is therefore wise to check with your vet as to which method he favours before inoculations are given. Inoculate your puppies as soon as they are old enough and maintain regular booster injections throughout the dog's life.

Please do not show a dog that is suffering with kennel cough. Apart from the fact that the dog will be feeling far from well, it is highly contagious and can be carried home by unsuspecting exhibitors, some of whom may have young litters.

ENTROPION

This is a condition affecting the eyelids, causing them to turn in. Consequently the eyelashes rub against the eyeball. Either the upper or the lower lids, or both, may be affected, in one or both eyes, and can cause the dog severe discomfort. The first sign may be a heavy tear-staining of the coat, running down the face from the eye. Although there can be several causes of this, entropion should certainly be considered as a possibility and veterinary advice sought.

Although this condition is operable, it is hereditary, and although the problem may be cured by medical intervention, it is going to recur in subsequent litters. Stock diagnosed as suffering – and they do suffer – from this condition should not be bred from. Entropion is a recessive fault, and if neither sire nor dam show signs of the disease but produce affected puppies, they must both be carriers. It is therefore unfair to blame one or the other parent.

SKIN COMPLAINTS

Itchy skins unfortunately seem to be the order of the day for many Bulldogs, and it is a fact that throughout the breed there does seem to be a tendency for puppies and adults alike suddenly to develop skin problems. Wet eczema can be a problem, as it develops extremely quickly and can spread with alarming speed. It seems to be triggered off, especially in hot or humid conditions, by the dog scratching at one particular spot, to the extent that a lesion is formed, which then starts to weep and in no time at all has turned into a wet patch of exposed raw skin. Although antihistamine will help in some cases, it does seem to be one of those problems which has to run its course before clearing up, and all we can do is to try and stop the area becoming infected.

Another problem quite commonly seen in the Bulldog is that of demodectic mange. This is frequently confused with the contagious sarcoptic mange, but in fact demodectic mange is not contagious, and is caused by a mite which lives deep in the layers of the skin. Although not always easy to diagnose, a skin scraping will normally tell whether or not this is the problem. Demodectic mange, unlike sarcoptic, does not normally cause irritation and usually shows itself as red patches, often on the tummy or exposed areas of skin. Although it is true to say that this problem is passed through the bitch line, as the mite crosses over from the bitch to the puppies during the first few days of suckling, it is not necessarily fair to blame the bitch for producing stock which is found to have this particular problem, and the reason for it seems to cause some confusion.

Most dogs have the demodectic mite as part of their natural make-up, and it will be found to be present in dogs of all breeds, also crossbreeds. The problem arises when the dog's immunity to the mite is insufficient to cope, and it is quite common to see the characteristic bare patches of skin on elderly dogs, or dogs whose natural immune system is breaking down due to some other reason. The inability to control this mite is hereditary and so it could just as easily have been passed down from the sire.

Demodectic mange is curable, and with regular baths most dogs respond well to treatment, and a recurrence, if treated properly, is not usual. The treatment prescribed by your veterinary surgeon will probably include a course of antibiotics to stop any secondary infection from establishing itself in the skin.

CHERRY EYE

This is the common name given to the prolapsed harderian gland, which is situated just below the inner corner of the eye. When this nictitating membrane prolapses it causes a swelling in the corner of the eye, not dissimilar in a severe case to the appearance of a cherry. At one time this problem would commonly be seen in show exhibits and it was not unknown for exhibitors to gently push the gland back into place, just prior to their class, hoping that it would stay there for the duration of the show. If the gland has been out for some time it will become dry and swollen. In any case, it is better to seek professional help. Although if caught in the early stages it is possible to replace the gland by closing the dog's eye, then gently putting a little pressure on the gland and pushing into the corner of the eye, in the majority of cases it will prolapse again by the following day and if this is the case there is little point in repeatedly putting it back.

Because of the Bulldog's placid temperament it is quite easy for the operation to remove the gland to be carried out under local anaesthetic, and in the twenty years that we have been associated with the breed, we have had probably twenty such operations done by various vets, and have never had one which required general anaesthetic, but you must be guided by your own vet. Although there is a certain risk of 'dry eye' when removing the gland completely, this is not something which we have experienced, and the operation to remove seems to be far more satisfactory than attempting to sew the gland into place – the advantage of this being that the tear gland in the third eyelid is retained, lessening the chance of 'dry eye' at a later date.

PARASITES

Internal Roundworms affect dogs of all ages and it is certainly a wise precaution to maintain a regular worming regime throughout the whole kennel. At Kingrock all of the kennel are wormed twice yearly. Bitches which have not been kept sufficiently wormed during pregnancy will often pass roundworm on to the unborn puppies, through the bitch's blood supply, and the damage that this can cause to the newborn whelps can be quite devastating, to the extent that in some cases the puppies will develop the condition known as 'fading puppy' syndrome, which actually is a term used to cover many conditions.

We take the worming of breeding stock very seriously and our 'in whelp' bitches are wormed with a preparation available from the vet, which is administered daily, from the fortieth day of gestation until two days after the litter is born. This regime has provided the best protection against a worm problem in puppies that we have found.

Roundworms look like small earthworms and can be very small or up to five or six inches in length. The tapeworm on the other hand tends to break off in small segments, whilst staying attached to the lining in the dog's stomach, and they show as rice-grain-like deposits in the faeces or around the dog's anus. The tapeworm is not seen as commonly as the roundworm and a vet will prescribe a suitable vermifuge.

External: Fleas are the most troublesome of the external parasites attracted by the dog. Although extremely common amongst the dog population, the social implications of having a flea-ridden member of the family has limited appeal and quite rightly so. Unfortunately any dog which visits the local park or attends dog shows, or in fact leaves the house, is going to be exposed at some time to these unwelcome little hitch-hikers, but by taking a few precautions you can make their choice of your dog as their 'Shangri-La' short-lived.

Flea collars are usually most effective, but some Bulldogs object to wearing a collar on a 'full-time' basis and will scratch them off. The aerosol sprays do seem to be the easiest and most effective way of keeping the house a 'flea-free zone', and we spray our dogs every couple of weeks or so throughout the summer months. A quick spray around the house with a product specifically designed for this purpose will make doubly sure.

Ticks are not so common as the flea, and are usually picked up on country walks. Although ticks are quite easy to see as they feed off their host, it is not a good idea just to pull the tick off. First apply surgical spirit to it, as this will lessen the chance of leaving the head of the tick imbedded in the dog's skin, where it could set up an infection. Then remove it.

CARE OF THE ELDERLY DOG

Generally speaking, and with a little luck, most Bulldogs will reach double figures and we have owned several champion studs who were still capable of siring litters, and did so, until well past their tenth birthdays.

A close eye should be kept on nails as the years creep on and the dog's exercise decreases.

Pay particular attention to the dewclaws, as they can so easily grow around and back into the pad.

Generally speaking, Bulldogs do not seem to suffer very much from tooth decay, but one should always be on the lookout for any sign of problems with teeth, as tooth-ache is such a wretched thing and your Bulldog is totally reliant on you noticing that he may be suffering.

It is important not to let the elderly Bulldog become obese. Bulldogs slow up naturally as they get older and the added burden of carrying surplus weight is one of the few age-related handicaps within our control. It may not be easy, but try to avoid giving fattening tit-bits. Give your oldies small pieces of apple as a treat – most will eat a variety of fruit, especially if they see you eating some as well. Also, most older dogs prefer to eat two or three small meals a day rather than one large meal.

Most Bulldogs are happy to poddle around the house and garden during their twilight years and, although some enjoy a short walk, most prefer to rely on motorised transport!

Each stage of a Bulldog's life will hopefully bring with it much joy and little pain, but it is a sad fact that the time may come when the quality of life, taken for granted in earlier times, may not be there and it is at this stage that your beloved Bulldog needs your devotion more than at any other. I have observed many instances of Bulldogs being allowed to carry on, even though in continual pain and discomfort, because the owners could not bring themselves to make the decision that we all dread. Of course it may happen that, when the time has come, your companion will pass away peacefully while sleeping, but if this is not to be, please be guided by your vet – although most owners know instinctively when the time has come.

Chapter Seven

THE BREED STANDARD

The Bulldog standard, first published by the Bulldog Club Inc. on May 27th 1875, has been the main reference point for many generations of Bulldog fanciers both at home and abroad. Apart from the change of weight, increased by five pounds for each sex during the early 1950s, the following standard is basically the original. In 1986 the English Kennel Club revised all of its breed standards and although the new version is adequately descriptive, it has lost much of the colour and charm of the breed's original standard. For this reason I have reproduced both the Bulldog Club Inc. and English KC standards.

'THE BULLDOG CLUB INCORPORATED' BREED STANDARD

GENERAL APPEARANCE: In forming a judgement on any specimen of the breed, the general appearance, which is the first impression a dog makes as a whole on the eye of the judge, should first be considered. Secondly, should be noticed its size, shape and make, or rather its proportions in the relation they bear to each other. No point should be so much in excess of the others as to destroy the general symmetry, or make the dog appear deformed, or interfere with its powers of motion, etc. Thirdly, its style, carriage, gait, temper, and its several points should be considered separately in detail, due allowance being made for the bitch, which is not so grand or as well developed as the dog.

The general appearance of the Bulldog is that of a smooth-coated, thick-set dog, rather low in stature, but broad, powerful and compact. The head strikingly massive, and large in proportion to the dog's size. The face extremely short. The muzzle very broad, blunt and inclined upwards. The body short and well-knit; the limbs stout and muscular. The hindquarters very high and strong but rather lightly made in comparison with its heavily made foreparts. The dog should convey an impression of determination, strength and activity, similar to that suggested by the appearance of a thick-set Ayrshire bull.

From its formation the dog has a peculiar heavy and constrained gait, appearing to walk with short, quick steps on the tips of its toes, its hind feet not being lifted high, but appearing to skim the ground, and running with the right shoulder rather advanced, similar to the manner of a horse in cantering.

HEAD AND SKULL: The skull should be very large – the larger the better – and in circumference should measure (round in front of the ears) at least the height of the dog at the shoulders. Viewed from the front it should appear very high from the corner of the lower jaw to the apex of the skull, and also very broad and square. The cheeks should be well rounded and extended sideways beyond the eyes. Viewed at the side, the head should appear very high, and very very short from its back to the point of the nose. The forehead should be flat, neither prominent nor over-hanging the face; the

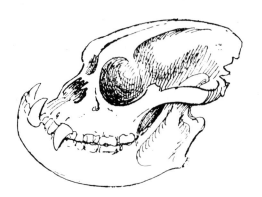

The skull of the Bulldog. This clearly shows the properties of the head, which can cause confusion to those who are not very familiar with the breed. This illustration shows the turn of underjaw, the amount by which the underjaw is undershot, the lay-back of nose, and the furrow.

skin upon it and about the head very loose and well wrinkled. The projections of the frontal bones should be very prominent, broad, square and high, causing a deep and wide indentation between the eyes, termed the 'stop'. From the 'stop' a furrow both broad and deep should extend up to the middle of the skull, being traceable to the apex. The face, measured from the front of the cheek bone to the nose, should be as short as possible, and its skin should be deeply and closely wrinkled. The muzzle should be short, broad, turned upwards and very deep from the corner of the eye to the corner of the mouth. The nose should be large, broad and black, and under no circumstances should it be liver coloured or brown; its top should be deeply set back almost between the eyes. The distance from the inner corner of the eye (or from the centre of the stop between the eyes) to the extreme tip of the nose should not exceed the length from the tip of the nose to the edge of the under lip. The nostrils should be large, wide and black, with a well-defined vertical straight line between them. The flews, called the 'chop', should be thick, broad, pendant and should join the under lip in front and quite cover the teeth. The jaws should be broad, massive and square, the

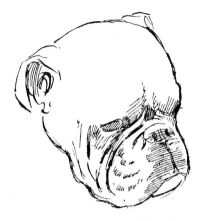

Good width and depth of foreface, but with a distinct lack of work (wrinkle) in the skull, which appears domed or apple-headed. It also lacks the desired furrow which should divide the skull evenly from stop to occiput.

The exact opposite. It shows a good skull, which is well-divided, and with more definition of the cheek. There is also good length from eye to ear. However, the foreface does not balance the head and looks deficient in strength, lacking the required padding of upper lip (cushion).

CORRECT: A perfect head, with good balance between skull and foreface, a defined stop, good nose placement and lay-back, and correct length overall.

lower jaw should project considerably in front of the upper and turn up. Viewed from the front, the various properties of the face must be equally balanced on either side of an imaginary line down the centre of the face.

EYES: The eyes seen from the front should be situated low down in the skull, as far from the ears as possible. The eyes and the 'stop' should be in the same straight line, which should be at right angles to the furrow. They should be as wide apart as possible, provided their outer corners are within the outline of the cheeks. They should be quite round in shape, of moderate size, neither sunken nor prominent, and in colour should be very dark – almost, if not quite, black, showing no white when looking directly forward.

EARS: The ears should be set high on the head – i.e. the front inner edge of each ear should (as viewed from the front) join the outline of the skull at the top corner of such outline, so as to place them as wide apart and as high and as far from the eyes as possible. In size they should be small and thin. The shape termed 'rose ear' is correct, and folds inward at its back, the upper or front edge curving over outwards and backwards, showing part of the inside of the burr.

MOUTH: The jaw should be broad and square and have the six small front teeth between the canines in an even row. The canine teeth or tusks wide apart. The teeth should not be seen when the mouth is closed. The teeth should be large and strong. When viewed from the front, the underjaw should be centrally under the upper jaw to which it should also be parallel.

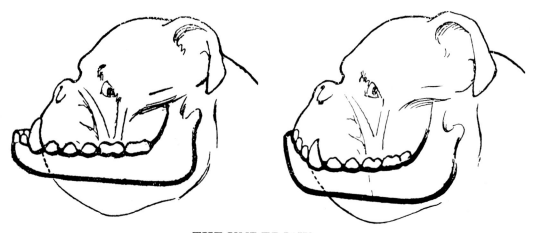

THE UNDERJAW

It is not always easy to determine whether or not a Bulldog has the correct underjaw without close examination. The correct 'sweep' of underjaw (formerly referred to as a 'carpet-bag' underjaw) is seldom found. This shows a common formation of underjaw which is flat and lacks any turn. Dogs with this type of underjaw usually lack depth of foreface, and will also show either their incisor or canine teeth when the mouth is closed.

This is another, but equally wrong conformation of underjaw. Here, the turn-up is confined to the front of the jaw; it can easily be mistaken as correct, without careful examination.

This underjaw gives the correct depth through the head, but lacks turn.

CORRECT: The correct turn of underjaw with the curve starting from the back of the jaw, and with the correct up-sweep. Close examination of the teeth gives a clear indication as to the shape of the underjaw. There must be sufficient curve to enable the jaw to be undershot, yet, at the same time, the teeth must be placed in the correct position so they are not visible when the mouth is shut.

NECK: Should be moderate in length (rather short than long) very thick, deep and strong. It should be well arched at the back, with much loose, thick and wrinkled skin about the throat, forming a dewlap on each side from the lower jaw to the chest.

FOREQUARTERS: The shoulders should be broad, sloping and deep, very powerful and muscular, and giving the appearance of having been 'tacked on' to the body. The brisket should be capacious, round and very deep from the top of the shoulders to its lowest part where it joins the chest, and be well let down between the forelegs. It should be large in diameter and round behind the forelegs (not flat sided, the ribs being well rounded). The forelegs should be very stout and strong, set wide apart, thick, muscular and straight, with well developed forearms, presenting a rather bowed outline, but the bones of the leg should be large and straight, not bandy or curved. They should be rather short in proportion to the hindlegs, but not so short as to make the back appear long, or detract from the dog's activity, and so cripple him. The elbows should be low and stand well away from the ribs. The pasterns should be short, straight and strong.

BODY: The chest should be very wide, laterally round, prominent and deep, making the dog appear very broad and short-legged in front. The body should be well ribbed up behind, with the belly tucked up and not pendulous. The back should be short and strong, very broad at the shoulders, and comparatively narrow at the loins. There should be a slight fall to the back close behind the shoulders (its lowest part), whence the spine should rise to the loins (the top of which should be higher than the top of the shoulders), thence curving again more suddenly to the tail, forming an arch – a distinctive characteristic of the breed – termed 'roach-back'.

HINDQUARTERS: The legs should be large and muscular, and longer in proportion than the forelegs, so as to elevate the loins. The hocks should be slightly bent and well let down, so as to be long and muscular from the loins to the point of the hock. The lower part of the leg should be short, straight and strong. The stifles should be round and turned slightly outwards away from the body. The hocks are thereby made to approach each other, and the hind feet to turn outwards.

FEET: The hind feet, like the fore feet, should be round and compact, with the toes well split up and the knuckles prominent. The fore feet should be straight and turn very slightly outwards, of medium size and moderately round. The toes compact and thick, being well split up, making the knuckles prominent and high.

TAIL: The tail, termed the 'stern', should be set on low, jut out rather straight, then turn downwards. It should be round, smooth and devoid of fringe or coarse hair. It should be moderate in length – rather short than long – thick at the root and tapering quickly to a fine point. It should have a downwards carriage (not having a decided upward curve at the end), and the dog should not be able to raise it over its back.

COAT: Should be fine in texture, short, close and smooth (hard only from the shortness and closeness, not wiry).

COLOUR: The colour should be whole or smut (that is, a whole colour with a black mask or muzzle). The only colours (which should be brilliant and pure of their sort) are whole colours, viz. – brindles, reds, with their varieties, fawns, fallows, etc., white and also pied (i.e. a combination of white with any other of the foregoing colours). Dudley, black and black with tan are extremely undesirable colours.

WEIGHT AND SIZE: The most desirable weight for the Bulldog is 55 pounds for a dog and 50 pounds for a bitch.

Although the scale of points is no longer included in the breed standard the following list shows how the 100 points were originally awarded.

MOUTH   **5**
Width and Squareness of Jaw   2
Projection and upward turn of Lower Jaw 2
Size and Condition of Teeth   1

CHOP   **5**
Breadth   2
Depth   2
Complete covering of Front Teeth   1

FACE   **5**
Shortness   1
Breadth   1
Depth   1
Shape and upward turn of Muzzle   1
Wrinkles   1

STOP   **5**
Depth   2
Breadth   2
Extent   1

SKULL   **15**
Size   5
Height   1
Breadth and Squareness   3
Shape   2
Wrinkles   4

EYES   **5**
Position   2
Size   1
Shape   1
Colour   1

EARS   **5**
Position   1
Shape   1.5
Size   1.5
Thinness   1

CHEST AND NECK		**5**
Length	1	
Thickness	1	
Arch	1	
Dewlap	1	
Width, Depth and Roundness	1	
SHOULDERS		**5**
Size	2	
Breadth	2	
Muscle	1	
BODY		**5**
Depth and Thickness of Brisket	2	
Capacity and Roundness of Ribs	3	
BACK ROACH		**5**
Shortness	2	
Width of Shoulders	1	
Shape, Strength and Arch at Loin	2	
FORE LEGS		**5**
Stoutness	1.5	
Shortness	1	
Development	1	
Feet	1.5	
HIND LEGS		**5**
Stoutness	1	
Length	1	
Shape and Development	2	
Feet	1	
SIZE		**5**
COAT		**5**
TAIL		**5**
GENERAL APPEARANCE		**10**
TOTAL		**100**

THE BRITISH BREED STANDARD.
Produced by The English KC

One of our oldest indigenous breeds, known as the national dog of Great Britain, and associated throughout the world with British determination and the legendary John Bull.

A delightfully ugly dog with his pugilistic expression, which belies a loving, affectionate nature to family and friends. He has a reputation for tenacity and is very courageous, strong and powerful. A little bit stubborn by nature, but good-tempered with children, of whom he is also fiercely protective. The impression he gives of being slow and sluggish is completely contradicted by the great bursts of speed which he can and does produce when the occasion demands.

His mood can be dignified, humorous or comical, and he has many endearing ways.

GENERAL APPEARANCE
Smooth-coated, thick-set, rather low in stature, broad, powerful and compact. Head massive, fairly large in proportion to size but no point so much in excess of others as to destroy the general symmetry, or make the dog appear deformed, or interfere with its powers of motion. Face short, muzzle broad, blunt and inclined upwards. Body short, well knit, limbs stout, well muscled and in hard condition. Hindquarters high and strong but somewhat lighter in comparison with heavy foreparts. Bitches not so grand or well developed as dogs.

CHARACTERISTICS
Conveys impression of determination, strength and activity.

TEMPERAMENT
Alert, bold, loyal, dependable, courageous, fierce in appearance, but possessed of affectionate nature.

HEAD AND SKULL
Skull large in circumference, should measure round (in front of ears) approximately height of dog at shoulder. Viewed from front appears very high from corner of lower jaw to apex of skull; also very broad and square. Cheeks well rounded and extended sideways beyond eyes. Viewed from side, head appears very high and short from back to point of nose. Forehead flat with skin upon and about head, loose and wrinkled, neither prominent nor overhanging face. Projections of frontal bones prominent, broad, square and high; deep, wide indentation between eyes. From stop, a furrow, both broad and deep extending to middle of skull being traceable to apex. Face from front of cheek bone to nose, short, skin wrinkled. Muzzle short, broad, turned upwards and very deep from corner of eye to corner of mouth. Nose and nostrils large, broad

and black, under no circumstances liver colour, red or brown; top set back towards eyes. Distance from inner corner of eye (or from centre of stop between eyes) to extreme tip of nose not exceeding length from tip of nose to edge of underlip. Nostrils large and wide with well defined vertical straight line between. Flews (chops) thick, broad, pendent and very deep, hanging completely over lower jaws at sides, not in front, joining underlip in front and quite covering teeth. Jaws broad, massive and square, lower jaw projecting considerably in front of upper and turning up. Viewed from front, the various properties of the face must be equally balanced on either side of an imaginary line down centre.

THE EXPRESSION

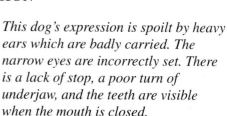

CORRECT: A nicely balanced head with a well-divided skull. The foreface is well-filled, with a good width and turn of underjaw, with good lines, all helping to create the correct 'sour' expression.

This dog's expression is spoilt by heavy ears which are badly carried. The narrow eyes are incorrectly set. There is a lack of stop, a poor turn of underjaw, and the teeth are visible when the mouth is closed.

Lack of foreface gives this dog an almost triangular head, which lacks strength and balance.

The disproportionate strength of the foreface on this dog gives an almost monkey-like expression and conveys a lack of intelligence.

This expression is rarely seen in the show ring today. The lack of underjaw, combined with the narrow foreface and protruding eyes, has a bad effect on the dog's expression. The upper lip is almost covering the underjaw, which is known in the breed as being 'frog-faced'.

EYES
Seen from front, situated low down in skull, well away from ears. Eyes and stop in same straight line, at right angles to furrow. Wide apart, but outer corners within the outline of cheeks. Round in shape, of moderate size, neither sunken nor prominent, in colour very dark – almost black – showing no white when looking directly forward.

EARS
Set high – i.e. front edge of each ear (as viewed from front) joins outline of skull at top corner of such outline, so as to place them as wide apart, as high and as far from eyes as possible. Small and thin. 'Rose ear' correct, i.e. folding inwards back, upper or front inner edge curving outwards and backwards, showing part of inside of burr.

MOUTH
Jaws broad and square with six small front teeth between canines in an even row. Canines wide apart. Teeth large and strong, not seen when mouth closed. When viewed from front under jaw directly under upper jaw and parallel.

NECK
Moderate in length (rather short than long), very thick, deep and strong. Well arched at back, with much loose, thick and wrinkled skin about throat, forming dewlap on each side, from lower jaw to chest.

THE EARS

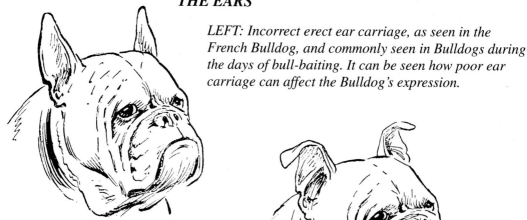

LEFT: Incorrect erect ear carriage, as seen in the French Bulldog, and commonly seen in Bulldogs during the days of bull-baiting. It can be seen how poor ear carriage can affect the Bulldog's expression.

BELOW: 'Button' ears, as seen in the Boxer. This ear carriage spoils the Bulldog's expression – probably more than any other – and gives the head a heavy, doleful appearance. Thick, heavy ears are passed on through certain lines, but, in fact, the button ear can sometimes be prevented by carefully sticking the ear into the correct position. This is only effective in young puppies, as once the shape of the ear is set, no amount of sticking will affect the final ear shape.

ABOVE: The 'tulip' ear is more commonly seen today, and often occurs when the ears are particularly small and thin. Some puppies go through a stage of 'flying' their ears while teething, but if this is carried on into adulthood it will be severely penalised in the show ring.

RIGHT: Correct. The 'rose' ear, which shows the head off to its best possible advantage. The skull appears longer and gives the correct expression.

FOREQUARTERS

Shoulders broad, sloping and deep, very powerful and muscular giving appearance of being 'tacked on' body. Brisket capacious, round and very deep from top of shoulders to lowest part where it joins chest. Well let down between forelegs. Large in diameter, round behind forelegs (not flat-sided, ribs well rounded). Forelegs very stout and strong, well developed, set wide apart, thick, muscular and straight, presenting rather bowed outline, but bones of legs large and straight, not bandy nor curved and short in proportion to hind legs, but not so short as to make back appear long, or detract from dog's activity and so cripple him. Elbows low and standing well away from ribs. Pasterns short, straight and strong.

THE BODY

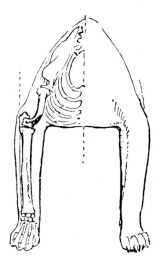

LEFT: This front lacks bone and is tight in shoulder. There is no depth or width of brisket, and the dog appears to be too tall.

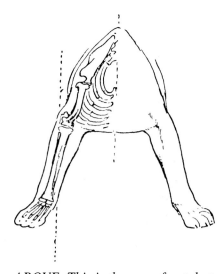

ABOVE: This is the same front, but it has been forced to give the appearance of better width. This positioning of the feet is commonly seen in the show ring, and, in fact, does little more than draw the judge's attention to the dog's lack of front. No matter how much your Bulldog lacks in front, it is far better to let him stand naturally.

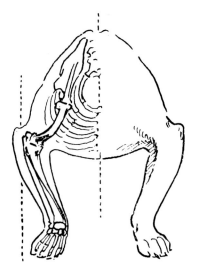

LEFT: This dog lacks shoulder. His width of front comes from an exaggerated turn of elbow, giving an appearance of weakness. With this type of front, the front feet turn out to compensate for the curved forearm. The poor conformation will show clearly on the move.

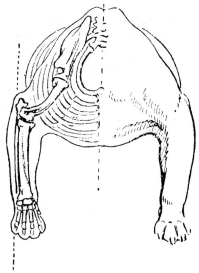

CORRECT: The perfect front with good width of shoulder, straight bone of the forearm, leading to strong pasterns and tight feet. A sufficient depth of brisket combined with a good turn of forearm ensures the correct positioning of the feet, with a slight turn outward.

CORRECT: The perfect front in conjunction with the correct head.

BODY
Chest wide, laterally round, prominent and deep. Back short, strong, broad at shoulders comparatively narrower at loins. Slight fall to back close behind shoulders (lowest part) whence spine should rise to loins (top higher than top of shoulder), curving again more suddenly to tail, forming arch (termed roach back) – a distinctive characteristic of breed. Body well ribbed up behind with belly tucked up and not pendulous.

HINDQUARTERS
Legs large and muscular, longer in proportion than forelegs, so as to elevate loins. Hocks slightly bent, well let down; leg long and muscular from loins to hock; short, straight, strong lower part. Stifles round and turned slightly outwards away from body. Hocks thereby made to approach each other and hind feet to turn outwards.

FEET
Fore, straight and turning very slightly outward; of medium size and moderately round. Hind, round and compact. Toes compact and thick, well split up, making knuckles prominent and high.

TAIL
Set on low, jutting out rather straight and then turning downwards. Round, smooth and devoid of fringe or coarse hair. Moderate in length – rather short than long – thick at root, tapering quickly to a fine point. Downward carriage (not having a decided upward curve at end) and never carried above back.

GAIT/MOVEMENT
Peculiarly heavy and constrained, appearing to walk with short, quick steps on tips of toes, hind feet not lifted high, appearing to skim ground, running with one or other shoulder rather advanced.

COAT
Fine texture, short, close and smooth (hard only from shortness and closeness, not wiry).

COLOUR
Whole or smut (i.e. whole colour with black mask or muzzle). Only whole colours (which should be brilliant and pure of their sort) viz., brindles, reds with their various shades, fawns, fallows etc., white and pied (i.e. combination of white with any of the foregoing colours). Dudley, black and black with tan highly undesirable.

SIZE
Weight: dogs: 25 kgs (55 lbs); bitches: 22.7 kgs (50 lbs).

FAULTS
Any departure from the foregoing points should be considered a fault and the seriousness with which the fault should be regarded should be in exact proportion to its degree.

NOTE: Male animals should have two apparently normal testicles fully descended into the scrotum.

Reproduced by kind permission of the English Kennel Club.

THE AMERICAN BREED STANDARD

(Standard for excellence of type in the Bulldog, as adopted by The Bulldog Club of America, 1896, and approved by The American Kennel Club. Revised July 20 1975).

GENERAL APPEARANCE, ATTITUDE, EXPRESSION, ETC.
The perfect Bulldog must be of medium size and smooth coat; with heavy, thick-set, low-slung body, massive short-faced head, wide shoulders and sturdy limbs. The

general appearance and attitude should suggest great stability, vigour and strength. The disposition should be equable and kind, resolute and courageous (not vicious or aggressive), and demeanour should be pacific and dignified. These attributes should be countenanced by the expression and behaviour.

GAIT
The style and carriage are peculiar, his gait being a loose-jointed, shuffling, sidewise motion, giving the characteristic 'roll'. The action must, however, be unrestrained, free and vigorous.

PROPORTION AND SYMMETRY
The 'points' should be well distributed and bear good relation one to the other, no feature being in such prominence from either excess or lack of quality that the animal appears deformed or ill-proportioned.

INFLUENCE of SEX
In comparison of specimens of different sex, due allowance should be made in favour of the bitches, which do not bear the characteristics of the breed to the same degree of perfection and grandeur as do the dogs.

SIZE
The size for mature dogs is about 50 pounds; for mature bitches about 40 pounds.

COAT
The coat should be straight, short, flat, close, of fine texture, smooth and glossy. (No fringe, feather or curl.)

COLOR of COAT
The color of coat should be uniform, pure of its kind and brilliant. The various colors found in the breed are to be preferred in the following order: (1) Red Brindle, (2) all other brindles, (3) solid white, (4) solid red, fawn or fallow, (5) Piebald, (6) inferior qualities of all the foregoing.

Note: A perfect piebald is preferable to a muddy brindle or defective solid color. Solid black is very undesirable, but not so objectionable if occurring to a moderate degree in piebald patches. The brindles to be perfect should have a fine, even and equal distribution of the composite colors. In brindles and solid colors a small white patch on the chest is not considered detrimental. In piebalds the color patches should be well defined, of pure color and symmetrically distributed.

SKIN
The skin should be soft and loose, especially at the head, neck and shoulders.

WRINKLES and DEWLAP

The head and face should be covered with heavy wrinkles, and at the throat, from jaw to chest, there should be two loose pendulous folds, forming the dewlap.

SKULL

The skull should be very large, and in circumference, in front of the ears, should measure at least the height of the dog at the shoulders. Viewed from the front, it should appear very high from the corner of the lower jaw to the apex of the skull, and also very broad and square. Viewed at the side, the head should appear very high, and very short from the point of the nose to occiput. The forehead should be flat (not rounded or domed), neither too prominent nor overhanging the face.

CHEEKS

The cheeks should be well rounded, protruding sideways and outward beyond the eyes.

STOP

The temples or frontal bones should be very well defined, broad, square and high, causing a hollow or groove between the eyes. This indentation, or stop, should be both broad and deep and extend up the middle of the forehead, dividing the head vertically, being traceable to the top of the skull.

EYES and EYELIDS

The eyes, seen from the front, should be situated low down in the skull, as far from the ears as possible, and their corners should be in a straight line at right angles with the stop. They should be quite in front of the head, as wide apart as possible, provided their outer corners are within the outline of the cheeks when viewed from the front. They should be quite round in form, of moderate size, neither sunken nor bulging, and in color should be very dark. The lids should cover the white of the eyeball, when the dog is looking directly forward, and the lid should show no 'haw'.

EARS

The ears should be set high in the head, the front inner edge of each ear joining the outline of the skull at the top back corner of skull, so as to place them as wide apart, and as high, and as far from the eyes as possible. In size they should be small and thin. The shape termed 'rose ear' is the most desirable. The rose ear folds inward at its back lower edge, the upper front edge curving over, outwards and backwards, showing part of the inside of the burr. (The ears should not be carried erect or prick-eared or buttoned and should never be cropped.)

FACE

The face, measured from the front of the cheekbone to the tip of the nose, should be extremely short, the muzzle being very short, broad, turned upwards and very deep from the corner of the eye to the corner of the mouth.

NOSE

The nose should be large, broad and black, its tip being set back deeply between the eyes. The distance from bottom of stop, between the eyes, to the tip of nose should be as short as possible and not exceed the length from the tip of nose to the edge of under lip. The nostrils should be wide, large and black, with a well-defined line between them. Any nose other than black is objectionable and brown or liver-coloured nose shall disqualify.

CHOPS

The chops or 'flews' should be thick, broad, pendant and very deep, completely overhanging the lower jaw at each side. They join the under lip in front and almost or quite cover the teeth, which should be scarcely noticeable when the mouth is closed.

JAWS

The jaws should be massive, very broad, square and 'undershot', the lower jaw projecting considerably in front of the upper jaw and turning up.

TEETH

The teeth should be large and strong, with the canine teeth or tusks wide apart, and the six small teeth in front, between the canines, in an even, level row.

NECK

The neck should be short, very thick, deep and strong and well arched at the back.

SHOULDERS

The shoulders should be muscular, very heavy, widespread and slanting outward, giving stability and great power.

CHEST

The chest should be very broad, deep and full.

BRISKET and BODY

The brisket and body should be very capacious, with full sides, well-rounded ribs and very deep from the shoulders down to its lowest part, where it joins the chest. It should be well let down between the shoulders and forelegs, giving the dog a broad, low, short-legged appearance. The body should be well ribbed up behind with the belly tucked up and not rotund.

BACK

The back should be short and strong, very broad at the shoulders and comparatively narrow at the loins. There should be a slight fall in the back, close behind the shoulders (its lowest part), whence the spine should rise to the loins (the top of which should be higher than the top of the shoulders), thence curving again more suddenly to the tail,

THE RIBS, CHEST AND LOIN

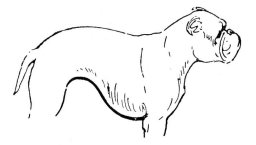

This dog lacks depth of chest and brisket, with a distinct lack of tuck-up at loin.

CORRECT: A deep brisket with good tuck-up.

forming an arch (a very distinctive feature of the breed), termed 'roach back' or, more correctly, 'wheel back'.

FORELEGS
The forelegs should be short, very stout, straight and muscular, set wide apart, with well developed calves, presenting a bowed outline, but the bones of the legs should not be curved or bandy, nor the feet brought too close together.

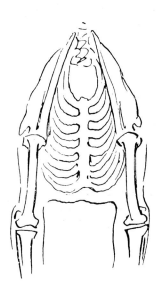

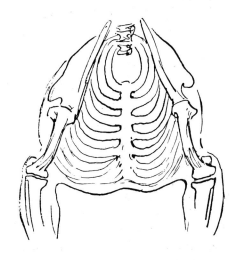

This front view shows the ribcage of a flat-sided dog, lacking the correct barrel rib.

CORRECT: The correct rib conformation with plenty of spring, giving adequate heart and lung room. This rib is necessary to obtain the correct 'pear-shaped' body.

THE BACK

This shows the equally wrong 'swamp' or 'sway' back. The topline gives an overall impression of weakness and is normally found on dogs that are too long in back. It is easy for newcomers to confuse a swampy-backed dog for one which exhibits the desirable 'roach' back.

Incorrect, flat topline.

I have always found this to be the most offensive of bad toplines, even though it is rarely seen in the breed. The 'camel' back differs from the roach mainly in the way in which the curve (which should start behind the wither) starts from the base of the neck. The gentle curve over the rump is also missing, giving an incorrect look to the croup.

CORRECT: The correct 'roach' or 'wheel' back, and although seldom seen to perfection in the show ring, it is the topline that all breeders should aim for. There is a slight fall just behind the wither, and then the spine rises in a curve to the loin, curving again, only more sharply, to the tail. This topline should also provide the correct low tail-set.

ELBOWS
The elbows should be low and stand well out and loose from the body.

HINDQUARTERS

  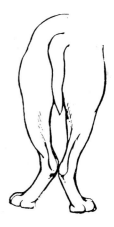

This shows the stilted hindquarter of a dog lacking in turn of hock, and straight in stifle.

Too much turn of hock, giving a weak appearance to the hindquarter.

This stance is referred to as being 'cow-hocked'. It is often, although not always, seen in dogs which are too high on the hock.

HIND LEGS
The hind legs should be strong and muscular and longer than the forelegs, so as to elevate the loins above the shoulders. The hocks should be slightly bent and well let down, so as to give length and strength from loins to hock. The lower leg should be short, straight and strong, with the stifles turned slightly outward and away from the body. The hocks are thereby made to approach each other, and the hind feet to turn outward.

A less common fault where the hindfeet turn in, referred to as 'pigeon-toed'. This is caused by the hock turning outwards and the stifle turning inwards – the exact opposite of the problem in the preceding illustration.

CORRECT: This shows a slight turning in of the hock, thereby turning the feet out slightly – as asked for in the Standard.

CORRECT: The correct hindquarter viewed in profile, clearly illustrating the bend of hock.

FEET

The feet should be moderate in size, compact and firmly set. Toes compact, well split up, with high knuckles and with short stubby nails. The front feet may be straight or slightly out-turned, but the hind feet should be pointed well outward.

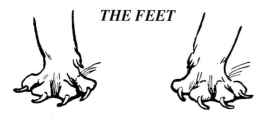

THE FEET

The 'splayed' foot is seen quite commonly in the show ring, and it is a most unattractive fault. The whole foot is weakened. The nails are likely to require far more attention as they are unlikely to wear evenly.

The 'hare foot' is not often seen in the breed. It usually accompanies weak pasterns.

The Standard asks for the feet to turn slightly outwards, but this is not the case in this illustration. The pasterns are weak, and the whole of the conformation of the front will be adversely affected.

CORRECT: This is the type of foot that all breeders should be striving for, with its well split-up, but thick, compact toes. The knuckles are prominent and high.

TAIL

The tail may be either straight or 'screwed' (but never curved or curly), and in any case must be short, hung low, with a decided downward carriage, thick root and fine tip. If straight, the tail should be cylindrical and of uniform taper. If 'screwed' the bends or kinks should be well defined, and they may be abrupt and even knotty, but no portion of the member should be elevated above the base or root.

THE TAIL

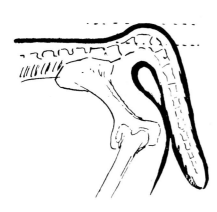

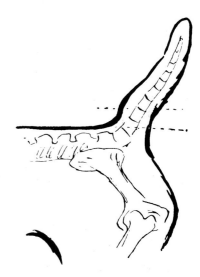

A flat topline invariably produces a high tail-set, as seen here. if the tail is carried downwards, or is of the screw type, it will not be as noticeable. However, it is equally incorrect, as a dog with this tail-set cannot possibly exhibit the correct 'roach' back.

The tail is carried gaily, which destroys the overall appearance of the Bulldog and is heavily penalised in the show ring. Thankfully, it is seldom seen today.

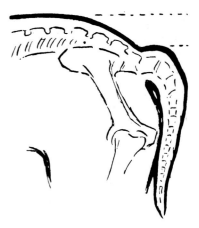

The screw tail, as seen here, is extremely common in the show ring and few judges penalise the fault heavily. Although this tail is not regarded as correct by the British Standard, the American Standard allows for either straight or screw tails.

CORRECT: The correct low-set tail with a good downward carriage, and tapering to a point. It is rarely seen in the show ring today, but it is by no means extinct. It is always a great treat when you do come across it.

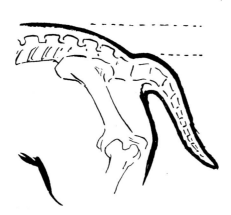

The same tail shown when the dog is excited. There should be no tendency to carry the tail gaily.

POINTS

GENERAL PROPERTIES		**22**
Proportion and symmetry	5	
Attitude	3	
Expression	2	
Gait	3	
Size	3	
Coat	2	
Color of coat	4	
HEAD		**39**
Skull	5	
Cheeks	2	
Stop	4	
Eyes and eyelids	3	
Ears	5	
Wrinkle	5	
Nose	6	
Chops	2	
Jaws	5	
Teeth	2	
BODY, LEGS, ETC.		**39**
Neck	3	
Dewlap	2	
Shoulders	5	
Chest	3	
Ribs	3	
Brisket	2	
Belly	2	
Back	5	
Forelegs and elbows	4	
Hind legs	3	
Feet	3	
Tail	4	
GRAND TOTAL		**100**

DISQUALIFICATION
Brown or liver colored nose.

Reproduced by kind permission of the Amerian Kennel Club.

ANALYSIS OF THE BREED STANDARD

Although the Bulldog of today may be a very different animal from the one used to satisfy the lust for blood sports which was so prevalent in early days, the Bulldog should still possess many of the characteristics sought by those fanciers involved with the design of the breed, for the Bulldog surely is, perhaps more than any other, a man-made breed.

GENERAL APPEARANCE

The standard asks for a dog of 'thick set' appearance and 'rather low in stature' and it is these very terms which have lent themselves to misinterpretation over the years, with resultant stock far too short on the foreleg and lacking the 'general symmetry' also required by the standard.

CHARACTERISTICS

'Conveys impression of determination, strength and activity' seems to be fairly self-explanatory but is sometimes not fully understood. A dog carrying too much weight does not give the impression of strength and would most certainly lose out on the 'activity' score. It is a big mistake to confuse fatness with substance, and an overweight Bulldog does not convey the required characteristics of the breed.

The perfect Bulldog, drawn by J. Hay Hutchinson, 1908.

TEMPERAMENT

The temperament of the Bulldog is seen by many as one of the breed's greatest assets, being fairly stolid and not easily roused to the point of aggression. It is for this reason that the Bulldog has become recognised as an ideal companion to children, but it is equally important to remember that it is unfair and indeed unwise to let children take advantage of his stoical nature. Although not a noisy breed, a Bulldog will generally let you know if there are strangers about and it is his very appearance which is usually the biggest deterrent to the would-be intruder.

HEAD and SKULL

The cheeks should extend beyond the eyes and be well rounded, otherwise the head will appear too narrow and chiselled. The head should appear, when viewed from the side, very short from the back to the point of nose. The head should appear balanced between skull and foreface with sufficient wrinkle covering the skull, evenly divided either side of an imaginary line running down the centre. This is most important and, in the occasionally seen fault of a wry face, a telltale sign is often that the nostrils are not the same size, as one will be narrowed by the slight twist of the face.

EYES

The positioning of the eyes is most important as it greatly affects the overall expression and, although they should be set wide apart, it is important that the eyes are not set so far apart as to make it impossible for him to look directly forward. The eyes and stop should be in a straight line and this is your guide as to whether a dog is up or down faced. The eyes should be round and as dark as possible, almost black is ideal. The pigmentation of the eyes is important and no white should show when the dog is looking directly forward. The eye rims are much more cosmetic if fully pigmented and this is greatly helped by the coat colour, as a patch over the eye will usually mean good dark eye rims.

NECK

Fairly self-explanatory in the standard, although many dogs these days do lack the required 'dewlap', which should hang in folds on each side of the throat.

FOREQUARTERS

The front of a Bulldog with its unique 'tacked on' shoulder is perhaps one of the most outstanding characteristics of the breed. The description in the standard is easy to follow but there is still some confusion for the layman, as it is widely believed that the front of the Bulldog should be bowed whereas, of course, the words in the standard are 'the bones of legs large, and straight, not bandy nor curved'.

BODY

Although the standard asks for a short back it should be remembered that the overall impression must be one of balance and a dog which is too short-coupled cannot 'flow' along the correct lines. Very often the ultra short-bodied dog will also lack length of neck, which not only affects the dog's movement but can also hamper his breathing. It is also not possible to attain the correct topline if the back is too short. Too much length of back is equally undesirable, if not so much from a health point of view, most certainly visually.

TAIL
Tail set and carriage is most important as it affects the dog's topline and therefore its general symmetry.

GAIT/MOVEMENT
The UK & US standards vary considerably over movement, with the US standard asking for the movement to be 'unrestrained, free and vigorous', whereas the UK standard stipulates that the movement should be 'peculiarly heavy and constrained'.

Bulldog movement is one of the most difficult points to understand fully and, as so few Bulldogs with correct movement appear in the show ring, it is almost impossible for the newcomer to acquire the correct 'eye' by observing dogs on the move. Most judges are concerned first and foremost with whether or not the dog is sound and well constructed. If the exhibit has something approaching good Bulldog movement, then this is indeed a bonus.

COAT
As described in the standard, 'fine texture, short, close and smooth'.

COLOUR
All colours except black are acceptable and in the US standard even black is acceptable 'if occurring to a moderate degree in piebald patches'. Whatever the coat colour, the pigmentation must be black.

SIZE
The UK standard asks for a weight of 25 kgs (55lbs) for dogs and 22.7 kgs (50lbs) for bitches. The US standard on the other hand asks for a weight of 50lbs for dogs and 40lbs for bitches. Certainly in the UK and, I suspect, in the US, this weight guide is often exceeded and in the UK a winning 55lb Bulldog male would be considered unusual. This is a great pity but many judges do seem to prefer the heavier animals and exhibitors will naturally try to produce stock which is going to appeal in the show ring.

NOTE
Although the 'note' in the UK standard states that 'male animals should have two apparently normal testicles fully descended into the scrotum', it is not a disqualification, as I believe it is in most countries, for the dog to have just one testicle descended, and there have been at least two UK champions which were not entire. This fault will be heavily penalised, though, by the judge and the dog would have to be truly outstanding to consider showing him.

DISQUALIFICATION
In the US standard a dog with a brown or liver coloured nose is to be disqualified.

Chapter Eight

IN THE SHOW RING

TRAINING FOR THE SHOW RING

If you have any intention of showing your Bulldog it is important to begin training for the ring at an early age. Use a plastic box approximately twenty inches by fourteen inches and ten inches high. Onto this glue a rubber mat similar to the ones used on a draining board. This stops the puppy from slipping. Putting the puppy on a box, even one just ten inches high, is enough to encourage the art of standing in the show position. Start training puppies in this way from the age of eight weeks, although only for five or ten minutes a day. It is surprising how quickly they learn. While they are standing, continually repeat the word 'stand' to them as the sound of your voice will help to reassure your puppy.

*Ch. Outdoors
Jubilant, bred by
George and Dora
Wakefield.
The Bulldog ring
is famous for its
personalities –
both human and
canine.*

Garwood.

ABOVE: Puppies must be taught to stand from an early age. Ch. Kingrock Freezo is pictured at seven weeks of age.

ABOVE: After a little practice your Bulldog should stand in the show position quite naturally. Ch. Kingrock Captain Christian is pictured at ten weeks of age.

Sw. Nor. Ch. Kingrock Tudor Flower in show pose, pictured at five months of age.

RINGCRAFT CLASSES

As soon as the course of vaccinations has been completed and the vet has given the all-clear for you to take your puppy out, it will help greatly with training if you can find a local 'ringcraft' class. These classes should not be confused with 'obedience classes', as they are very different and are concerned purely with those dogs who will ultimately be shown.

Most large towns have at least one ringcraft class running each week and either your vet or the secretary of the local canine society will probably be able to tell you where they are held and at what time.

If you have not shown before, the classes can seem a little daunting, but remember that all

Frymad Wellington handled by owner/breeder Yvonne Franklin. The judge (in this case, Arthur Rowe) must be able to make a close examination of the Bulldog's mouth.

Hartley.

Ch. Merriveen Halcyon Daze at the Bulldog of the Year competition, with handler Pat Meredith. The judge, Les Cotton, is 'going over' the dog to assess conformation.

Hartley.

of the people there started in the same way and many of them will be newcomers to the hobby also. Although I take our puppies along as soon as they are old enough, I do not normally actually take part in the lessons for a week or two. I prefer to allow the puppy to just soak up the atmosphere and, at this stage, it is the socialising aspect and getting the puppy accustomed to being in a confined area with a lot of other dogs which is most important.

If you have been to dog shows to watch the Bulldog judging you will already have some idea as to ring procedure but if not, this will be explained by one of the instructors at the ringcraft lesson. There may be other Bulldogs attending the classes and of course those with the same breed are instantly drawn to one another. If there are no other Bulldog owners, it will help if one of the instructors is familiar with the breed and is therefore aware of the positioning and stance of the Bulldog.

Bulldogs are meant to stand foursquare in the show ring and are always stood facing the judge, as opposed to most other breeds, which are stood sideways on. During the training the dogs will be moved up and down, usually, although not always, on a rubber mat. It is most important that your puppy is encouraged to do this without pulling on the lead. This breed is not shown on a tight lead. Each year I see several very nice puppies which are either unplaced or placed well down the line simply because of bad handling, making it impossible for the judge correctly to assess the animal. Ringcraft lessons are the place for such antics, not the show ring.

MATCHES

Most ringcraft organisations will also organise monthly matches. These are licensed by the Kennel Club and are for puppies over six months of age. The match is a very informal competition but that is not to say it is not taken seriously. As well as being an ideal starting block for new exhibitors to get some idea of the feeling of being in competition, it also serves as an ideal training ground for novice judges. All of us here at Kingrock, including our kennel manageress, are championship show judges and we all started our judging careers at local canine society match meetings – although longer ago than any of us choose to remember!

A match is conducted on a knock-out basis with just two dogs entering the ring at a time and the judge deciding which of the two will go forward to the next round. This is the only type of competition judged in this manner. At all other shows the dogs are entered in classes and all dogs entered in a particular class enter the ring at the same time.

One question you will often be asked by instructors at ringcraft classes who are not familiar with the breed is: 'Do you look in their mouths?' The confusion comes about because some of the flat-faced breeds do not have their mouths examined during judging; but in the case of the Bulldog the answer is a definite yes, so it is essential to get a youngster accustomed to this. Bulldog breed judges place a lot of importance on the mouth, and there are very definite requirements in the Standard as to the mouth's construction and dentition.

GAITING

When you are asked to move your Bulldog up and down the ring, try to remember that it is not a race and, for the correct Bulldog rolling movement to be shown to advantage, a steady speed should be maintained. The correct speed will be learnt with practice by both dog and handler, but in the early days many handlers tend to rush their exhibit and thereby spoil the dog's overall balance on the move.

Not only is ringcraft good for the dog but it can be a meeting point for those with a common interest; and many friendships which have lasted over several decades have started at such events.

RULES AND REGULATIONS OF SHOWING

The rules and regulations involving the showing of dogs are extremely complex and vary considerably throughout the world. The ultimate goal of most exhibitors is that of attaining the title of champion for their exhibit and, again, rules for achieving this vary greatly.

Ch. Olakin Nero, with owner/handler Les Howell, judged by Chris Thomas at the Bulldog of the Year competition.
Some dogs become 'old hands' in the art of showing, and pose themselves to advantage without assistance from the handler.

Kingrock Commander In Chief: The Bulldog is a difficult dog to handle, but top American professional handler Alan Levine makes it look easy.

Ashbey.

In the UK the title of champion is awarded to any dog which wins three KC challenge certificates under three different judges, with at least one of these awarded after the dog's first birthday. Challenge certificates are of course only awarded at championship shows and, as only one is awarded to each sex at any show, the competition for this illustrious award is always keen. The award of Junior Warrant is won on a points system and given at both championship and open shows but must be attained during the dog's Junior career, between twelve and eighteen months of age. Deciding which class your dog is eligible for can be somewhat daunting, as the qualification in the UK varies between Open and Championship shows. Wherever possible, go in age-restricted classes such as Minor Puppy six to nine months, Puppy six to twelve months and Junior six to eighteen months. The restrictions for entering classes is printed clearly in the show schedule which accompanies your entry form.

BECOMING A CHAMPION IN THE US
In the United States the system varies somewhat as points are the basis used for achieving champion status. As in the UK, the sexes are divided, and at least three different judges are required to give the requisite number of points (fifteen) to make a champion. The championship points are given for Winners Dog and Winners Bitch and the number of points given at a particular show will depend on such things as the number of dogs competing in your breed. The number of points varies in different parts of the country, but a list is printed in the catalogue for every show. The maximum number of points that it is possible to win at one show is five, and this would be considered to be a major. Any win from between three and five points constitutes a major and to become a champion, a dog must win at least two majors under different judges.

The classes in the United States are:

Puppy: The dog or bitch must be six months of age or older but no more than twelve months. Open only to puppies that were whelped in the USA or Canada and are not champions. At large shows the puppy entry will be split into six to nine months and nine to twelve months, slightly different to the UK classification of six to nine months (minor puppy and six to twelve months (puppy).

Novice: This is a class for dogs and bitches, six months of age or older, whelped in the USA or Canada, that have not won, prior to the close of entries, three first prizes in the novice class, or a first prize in Bred-by-Exhibitor, American bred or open class, nor one or more points toward a champion title.

American Bred: This class is open to any Bulldog (except champions) six months of age or older which was whelped in the United States, by a mating which took place there.

Bred by Exhibitor: Open to any dog which was whelped in the USA, is six months of age or older, is not a champion and which is owned wholly or in part by the person or by the spouse of the person who was the breeder or one of the breeders of record. The handler must also be an owner or immediate family of the owner.

Open: A class for any dogs six months of age or over. This is the only class which an imported Bulldog may enter.

Winners Dog and Winners Bitch: After the judging of a sex, all of the first-prize winners

South African Ch. Roseneath Emil of Ravenmoor, handled by Robert McNeilie, winning Best in Show at the Northern Transvaal Bulldog Club Championship Show in 1992. Emil was bred by George and Julia van Rooyen and is owned by Percy and Margaret Bevan.

Finland's 1991 Bulldog Show BIS line-up (pictured left to right): BOS Admirabull Cream Cracker with owner/breeder Christine Mattila, judge Les Thorpe from the UK, and BIS Fin. and Est. Ch. Tretun Bustersam of Kingrock with owner, Ari Hyvonen.

must compete in this class. The Reserve winner is selected immediately after the Winner.

Best of Breed Competition: This is limited to champions or recently qualified champions and Winners dog and bitch, together with any undefeated dogs which have been shown only in non-regular classes. All compete for Best of Breed or Best of Variety.

Best of Winners: If the Winners dog or Winners bitch earns BoB or BoV it automatically becomes BoW; otherwise they will be judged together for BoW after the judging of BoB or BoV.

THE ROLES OF THE JUDGE AND THE HANDLER

The judge, whether a breed specialist or an all-rounder, is trying to evaluate your dog. This is done by comparing all the dogs in the class and deciding in which order they should be placed. As a handler, it is your task to try to show the dog to advantage and to disguise as many faults as possible. This ability is what makes the difference between a good and a bad handler. It is worth bearing in mind that no dog is perfect and, if you can master the art of showing off the exhibit's virtues while, at the same time, hiding the dog's faults, you are on the right road to becoming a handler worthy of note.

As you learn more about the breed, and more particularly the breed Standard, the easier it will become to decide where a particular dog can be improved by clever handling. Of course the breed judge is constantly on the lookout for the faults which are, to some extent, disguisable by the handler, whereas the all-rounder may be more concerned with the dog as a whole and may be more inclined to miss the minor defects which can only be found on closer scrutiny.

Although showing in varieties can be great fun, as one becomes more involved in the breed, the urge to learn how your Bulldog compares with others of the same breed will grow. Whether one starts off at open shows, or jumps in at the deep end by entering championship shows, it is ultimately the wins in breed classes that will tell you how good a specimen of the breed your dog is from a show point of view. I stress 'from a show point of view' because, do remember, the dog you take home with you at the end of the day is the same one you arrived with – win, lose or draw. If you feel in any way differently towards your dog because you fail to go home with a prize, then shows are not for you.

Chapter Nine

BREEDING

THE STUD DOG.

Great achievements in the show ring are not in themselves enough to qualify a dog as a suitable candidate for stud work, although more often than not this initially creates the demand for a particular dog.

It should be remembered that a dog's dominance over the opposition in the show ring is no indication of his potential to dominate as a sire. Some of the breed's most outstanding show specimens, even when mated to some of the country's best producing bitches, have proved unable to sire stock which is any better than 'run of the mill'.

A dog's show career, although important, is only a small part of a much larger picture that one should try to build up before deciding on the suitability of a particular male.

CHOOSING A STUD DOG

One trap often fallen into by the newcomer is that of trying to correct one fault by introducing another: for example, mating a bitch which is rather short on the leg to a dog which is rather high, in the belief that one will counteract the other. This is of course incorrect and in fact such a mating would be far more likely to produce puppies which exhibit the fault of each parent – some too high on the leg and some too short. It should also be remembered that all the puppies would still be carrying the faults of both parents even if you were lucky enough to produce one of correct leg length from this mating.

It is far wiser to use a dog of the correct height, as some puppies tend to resemble each parent and on this basis the chance of producing the correct height in at least some of the puppies is much greater. They would also only be carrying one height fault, the one for shortness, inherited from their dam.

The best decisions regarding breeding programmes are usually based on pedigrees. Although the dog 'on floor' is taken into account, the final decision will ultimately rest on that single piece of paper which, if interpreted correctly, will tell you so much about the dog's potential to reproduce the qualities you desire.

If you are fairly new to the breed and, as yet, pedigrees mean very little, there is still much you can do to help ensure the right choice of dog. To begin with, steer away from the

Ch. Beechlyn Golden Nugget of Denbrough, owned by Dennis Shaw and bred by Joe Fox. He is the UK's breed record holder with 42CCs.

Fin. Ch. Kingrock Stonewall Jackson, a son of Ch. Kingrock Captain Christian.

younger dogs who have not yet had the opportunity to prove their worth at stud. These youngsters are better left to those with a deeper knowledge of the breed.

This is not the case with a dog who has been available at stud for a season or two. Carefully study his progeny in the show ring and the breeding of the bitches he has mated, and if any are of these are similarly bred to your own bitch, pay particular attention to the resulting puppies. The longer a dog has been at stud the easier it will be to assess his potential as a sire.

Also take note of any stud dogs that the more established kennels are using regularly, as these breeders are continually on the lookout for that prepotent male, who seems to come along every so often, who is capable of producing something special in almost every litter with seemingly little regard to the bitch's breeding.

It is a fact that not all top show specimens are going to be well bred and it does happen that occasionally a flyer will be produced in a quite ordinarily bred litter. When this does occur, invariably one finds that the siblings do not bear any resemblance to the winner and, in fact, are often of a completely different type. This situation does seem to occur more in the outcross litter, with the lack of breeding showing in the next generation, when the ability to pass on the qualities of the sire or dam in question is lost. This is just one of the advantages of line-breeding as opposed to out-crossing. This is of course assuming that the

Ch. Kingrock Captain Christian with one of his litters. Three of these puppies went on to become Champions.

line-bred pedigree is based on a producing line. One of the fundamental rules when considering the use of a stud dog is to establish, with as great a degree of certainty as possible, that he is not likely to pass on any major hereditary faults. This applies to any breed but even more so with a breed as complex as the Bulldog.

Decisions made by Bulldog breeders today will determine the legacy left to future generations. Problems we now face within the breed have been handed down to us by those breeders who chose to overlook them, sometimes even regarding them as acceptable in the breed, rather than trying to eradicate them. If no attempt is made to breed out faults as soon as they manifest themselves, within a surprisingly short space of time they will have become endemic. This should be borne in mind when choosing a stud, for if the main considerations governing the choice are financial or geographical rather than suitability, the whole breed will ultimately suffer as a result.

In Bulldogs particularly, where the demand for puppies is fairly constant, there is always the temptation to use a stud simply because he lives just around the corner or because he is owned by a friend. This really is not the way to start to develop a line and is a terribly false economy. Even so, many prefer to find this out the hard way and, as a consequence, countless litters of poorly-bred puppies are produced each year to help flood the pet market.

INFLUENTIAL STUD DOGS

Ch. Aldridge Advent Gold, owned and bred by Les and Ellen Cottton.

Garwood.

Ch. Quintic Amos at Ocobo, owned by Pat and Norman Davis, bred by Pat Perkins.   *Hartley.*

Ch. Aldridge Aristocrat of Brandywell, owned by Jean and Bill Cartwright, bred by Les and Ellen Cotton.

Hartley.

Ch. Isgraig Red Baron, owned and bred by Bill Roberts.

Hartley.

Ch. Ocobo Skipper, owned and bred by Pat and Norman Davis.

USING YOUR OWN DOG AT STUD

Many newcomers to the breed, having paid what they may consider to be a large sum of money for their first Bulldog, decide erroneously that if he is worth that much then he must be good enough to use at stud.

The fact that a pedigree may be ablaze with champions is no guarantee that the dog will be of any use in a breeding programme, for if he is from an outcross mating – that is where there is no common ancestry in his sire and dam's breeding – the likelihood is that he will not be as prepotent as would be the case if he were linebred. It should also be remembered that if the dog has not been successful in the show ring he will be unknown to breeders and therefore in little demand.

Even those breeders with little or no involvement in the show ring usually have a definite preference for a stud with an illustrious show career behind him and, better still, a champion, as this will create more demand for his offspring.

Another reason often put forward for using a pet dog at stud is that it would be good for him to become a father, even if just the once, almost implying that this will give him a more responsible attitude to life. Here the old adage of 'what you haven't had you won't miss' is completely appropriate.

Although it is quite true to say that many stud dogs are kept successfully as family pets, the majority live a kennel life and can be difficult to housetrain. Another major consideration before embarking on stud work is whether you can be sure of maintaining a steady supply of bitches to the dog. Is there a successful kennel nearby to whom those requiring a stud dog may prefer to go? Does your dog have a brother winning well in the show ring, or at stud in the hands of a well-known stud handler? These things should be taken into account. The pet dog given just an occasional opportunity for use will often not settle as a result and it is certainly not unknown for stud work to completely change a dog's character.

For these reasons please think very seriously before considering using your dog at stud for the first time – but if you still believe that his use is justified, read on.

PREPARING A DOG FOR STUD WORK

Assuming that you have overcome the first hurdles and that your dog's pedigree, as far as you are aware, carries no serious hereditary faults, the next questions are – how old must he be before commencing stud work and how often can he be used after that?

Not all dogs mature at the same age and although I, normally, would not attempt to use a Bulldog before the age of ten months, this is a generalisation, and we have had successful matings with dogs as young as seven months. Others have been well past their first birthday before showing any interest.

It is important to remember that stud work should be regarded as something enjoyable, particularly by the young dogs, and not something which sends them cowering away, as is commonly seen when those first all-important matings having been conducted badly. Poor handling can quite easily affect a dog's stud work for life and many good dogs have been ruined at stud by the handler's incompetence.

Bulldogs are not the easiest breed to handle at stud but neither are they the most difficult.

The mating stand: This is a simple device, but it can make stud work far more manageable. The wooden base measures 3ft 6ins by 2ft. The upright is 9ins high to the bottom of the support, and the curved section measures 13ins across. During a mating the curved support is covered with a piece of thick padding, making sure that the ends of the support are not exposed. The upright is adjustable, but this height is generally suitable for most stud dogs.

However, with particularly tall bitches (or short dogs), a block of wood, similar in shape to a telephone directory, can be used for the dog to stand on.

With the correct attitude a Bulldog mating should be no more troublesome to effect than that of any other breed.

There are several things to bear in mind. One is that, although the weight difference between a dog and bitch in the Standard is just five pounds, in reality the difference is often greater. It is not unusual to find males weighing as much as twenty pounds more than the bitches, which, for a fairly low-to-ground and compact breed, is quite considerable. For this reason we have, from the earliest days, used what is commonly referred to in the breed as a mating stand (a fairly self-explanatory term). It is an extremely simple device designed to help support the bitch during what can sometimes be a quite lengthy mating. This is not the only way to effect a mating and some stud handlers prefer to have the bitch over their knee (an old and tested method) but, whatever method is employed, it will generally be found to be the case that the bitch requires additional support.

Another point is that it is not unusual for Bulldog bitches to be quite aggressive at this time, but it is extremely important to ascertain that this aggressiveness is due to a natural reluctance to receive the dog and not because the bitch has not yet reached, or has passed, the correct stage of oestrus for a suitable mating to occur. If one is confident that the correct time has been reached, then the next priority must be to ensure the stud dog's protection, as not only could a poorly managed mating result in the dog being badly bitten, it could also unnerve a young dog, affecting future stud work for some time and, in some cases, indefinitely. For this reason the smooth running of those early matings for a young dog is imperative and, if the help of an experienced Bulldog stud handler is available, this should be gratefully accepted.

It is essential to make sure that you have adequate help when first attempting stud work with a young dog. I have always advocated having as few people as possible present, stressing that it is unfair to expect a young dog to perform stud work if surrounded by an entourage of onlookers. But it is equally important to ensure that, when the time comes to assist, as it will, there are enough willing hands.

We have found that three people are necessary to manage adequately. If the mating stand is employed – and we have not carried out a mating without it for over twenty years – one person is engaged to hold the bitch, with the use of a leather collar. The second person is there simply to steady the dog once he has mounted the bitch, and this person is positioned to one side of the stand. The third, and the position which is preferably taken by an experienced stud handler, ensures that the dog enters the bitch correctly and with as little distress to her as possible. It is often the case that a young dog will need to lifted into position on the bitch's back for the first couple of matings. It is preferable to do this rather than spend time trying to encourage the dog into position, very often upsetting the bitch in the process. It is most important to remember that the quicker the mating can be effected, the less the likelihood of either party becoming frightened.

THE MATING

Unlike other breeds, the tie is not normally expected and therefore the dog will remain in the mounted position throughout the duration of the mating, normally around fifteen minutes, although some dogs do prefer to stand to the side, which is also more comfortable for the bitch. In most breeds the dog is prevented from pulling away from the bitch by the swelling of the 'posterior gland' which is located at the base of the dog's penis. This would normally enlarge within the bitch, but in most cases with Bulldog matings, this gland remains just outside. Once the dog has entered the bitch, it will swell rapidly, thus enabling the stud handler to hold the dog in the correct position for the duration of the mating.

For this reason it is imperative to get a young dog used to being handled. He will come to rely heavily on his handler to ensure that the mating is conducted in such a way that no harm will befall either of the dogs involved. An unsupervised mating should never be allowed, as this could result in serious injury to both parties.

When the dog is ready to withdraw, the posterior gland will lessen in size and the dog will show that he is ready to draw away from the bitch. Trying to turn the dog during such a mating would probably be unsuccessful and result in him slipping out. It is a fallacy that it is necessary to get a tie to ensure a good mating as, in twenty years and literally hundreds of matings at Kingrock, we have never had a tied mating.

This is from choice, as we have not found it necessary and, if there is a problem during the mating due to excessively hot weather or some other reason, it is possible to separate the dog and bitch if they are not tied.

It is very important to remember that Bulldog matings are conducted in this way because virtually no bitches will stand unassisted, therefore it is extremely important to ensure the bitch is ready to receive the dog. If you are in any doubt, please ask someone experienced with stud work to tell you her correct day. If a good mating is achieved, repeat the mating two days later. In some breeds this would be considered unnecessary but in a breed which has a fairly high degree of 'misses' it increases your chances of success.

MEDICAL PRECAUTIONS

Although I do not insist that all bitches are checked for infection before visiting a stud dog, always check the bitch over before the mating starts. A cotton bud inserted just inside the vulva will indicate the amount of colour being shown and, even more importantly, whether the discharge is clean and showing no sign of infection. Bitches who have a history of missing are always recommended to go onto a prescribed course of antibiotics as soon as colour starts to show

Our stud dogs do not receive any medication on a regular basis as they do have a certain amount of built-in resistance to infection. However, when the dog's system cannot cope with an infection, this is usually indicated by a greenish discharge from the penis. It would then be wise to let your vet take a specimen in order to set up a sensitivity test, thus enabling the correct antibiotic to be prescribed.

Although we give a multi-vitamin additive to our stud dogs, their basic diet is the same as the other dogs'. It is most important not to let a working stud become overweight.

It is also worth considering, for the sake of the dog and bitch, trying to arrange evening matings during spells of warm weather. Bitches that are boarding with us are mated early in the morning during the summer months. This can also help from a kennel maintenance point of view, as our stud dogs are only used on an empty stomach, so an early mating, before the first feed, does not interfere with the feeding regime. Dogs that have a visiting bitch in the evening are given just a light breakfast.

Please remember that the life of a kennel stud dog does not need to be one of continual solitude. Most of our own studs have enjoyed the company of a bitch (which obviously must be removed during seasons), and I must admit the stud dogs do tend to be rather spoilt by the kennel staff as they are often great   personalities.

Unlike the brood bitch whose active part in a breeding programme is dictated by number of litters and age, the stud dog can contribute over a much longer period of time. Several of our champions have remained at stud until well past the age of ten, but this is only a generalisation and it would be unfair to expect a dog to remain at stud when his interest in such matters has waned.

THE BROOD BITCH.

One phrase which is repeated time and time again is that the strength of a kennel lies in its bitches – and how true that has proved to be!

I have found over the years that the majority of people looking for their first Bully pup will invariably want a bitch, although on closer questioning the reason for this decision is not always clear. Often it is simply because bitches have always been kept as pets within the family or, simply, they have been told that bitches make better pets. Whatever the reasoning, the demand for bitch puppies usually outweighs that for dogs – and generally speaking there are more dog puppies born each year than bitches, which tips the balance still further.

The majority of first-time buyers have little interest in breeding when making their purchase and, because of this, pay little attention to the puppy's pedigree. In a great many instances these same people will, in twelve months time, be looking around for a suitable sire for their potential brood. In the majority of cases this is done in total innocence, and at

See Threepio of Kingrock: Kingrock's first Best in Show winner, and an outstanding brood bitch for the kennel. Bred by Glyn Lake in 1977.

the time of purchase the thought of Bulldog breeding could not have been further from the buyer's mind. But time passes and friends start to remark on how nice it would be for the bitch to have a litter, or maybe the children start pressurising mum and dad into letting the dog start a little family of her very own. Whatever the reason, the puppy bought originally as a pet has a very different future in store, if certain plans come to pass.

MAKING AN INFORMED DECISION

It may be that you have been lucky and your first purchase was suitable as a pet or as a brood bitch, but this is not always the case, and before plans are set into action there are several things to take into account. When you bought your puppy, did the breeder give any reason for letting her go purely as a pet? Very often, if a breeder is particular about which of their stock is bred from, a Kennel Club endorsement will be placed on the registration form stopping the registration of progeny from this particular bitch. When you check your registration document any endorsements will be clearly shown and only the breeder of the puppy may have these endorsements removed – although if the breeder saw fit to put them there in the first place the likelihood is that they will not wish the bitch to be bred from and, if she was bought purely as a pet, you must respect the breeder's wishes.

If you do not have registration papers you should contact the bitch's breeder before considering breeding. There may be a problem which will make it impossible to register the litter, and an unregistered litter will be of very little value and should not be considered.

Ideally, before purchasing your first bitch and embarking on a breeding programme, a great deal of time will have been spent studying pedigrees and show catalogues to get some idea of which lines are proving to be the most successful. Although this is by no means a fail-safe way of acquiring top-draw stock, it does give some indication of the way the different lines develop and which ones keep their early promise.

Joining a breed club can also be most helpful. Attending the various functions and shows can be an ideal way of getting to know the breeders, who may seem rather unapproachable at the more serious championship shows, where they very often have too much on their minds to want to answer questions about breeding programmes. Generally one will find that established breeders, if approached in the correct way, will be most helpful and it is only through talking to such people that the newcomer can start to learn the basics of what is an extremely complicated breed.

CHOOSING A BROOD BITCH
When a decision has been made about which kennel you want your foundation bitch to come from, the next step will be to contact the kennel owner. It is at this stage that the formation of a good line can be made or lost. It must be accepted that the possibility of a bitch puppy of suitable breeding being available at just the time that you are looking for one is rather remote. It is now that all of the hard work of deciding on the right line goes up in smoke if the temptation to buy from someone with stock available, regardless of the breeding, is too much and a puppy of little more than pet quality is purchased to form the basis of your breeding programme, a move which would probably set you back ten years. Of course the readily available puppy is tempting, especially when the voice on the end of the telephone at the kennel you had intended buying from tells you that there will be nothing available for two or three months, which seems a lifetime away; but please be patient or you could regret it for a long time. It must mean something that the kennel you wanted stock from has nothing available and the other has stock ready to go but no purchasers!

Always bear in mind that it is not necessary to the health of the bitch for her to have a litter and, when you take into account the hours of work involved as well as the financial costs, including feeding and veterinary bills, there is really no purpose in mating your bitch other than wanting something home-bred for yourself. Before you mate your bitch please check as thoroughly as possible that she is free from hereditary complaints and is of good enough type to benefit the breed by producing more of a similar type.

THE IMPORTANCE OF TIMING
Assuming you have a bitch of suitable quality for breeding and the paperwork is all in order, including her transfer into your name, the next question is: how old must she be before her first litter? Generally speaking it should not be before her second season. This is only a

generalisation, as it depends greatly on when the bitch has her first season and how often the seasons then follow.

As a rule we will not mate a bitch under one year of age and, as Bulldog bitches tend to have their first season between the ages of six and nine months and then at roughly six-month intervals, the correct time generally coincides with their second season. If a bitch is particularly slow to mature or has a setback which affects her development, then it is far better to wait another six months than risk the bitch and her puppies by trying for a litter too early.

Another factor to bear in mind is the whelping date. It is very easy to mate a bitch and then find that she is due to whelp when it is most inconvenient. Remember that rearing a bulldog litter is a very time-consuming experience and arrangements will have to be made to enable constant supervision of the newly born litter.

When the bitch is due in season it is a good idea to keep an eye on her, as most bitches will show a degree of puffiness around the vulva and, for some, this will be apparent some time before they actually come into season. It is well worth swabbing the bitch each day with a piece of cotton wool as, particularly with young ones, it is easy to miss the first day or two of the season, making the working-out of correct mating days more difficult.

Bulldogs seem to differ from other breeds in many ways and one is with regard to establishing the correct day of mating by the tailing off or pinking of colour. Most bitches will show a blood-red discharge from the start of their season: this should be clean in appearance with no smell. As the season progresses the vulva will normally become more swollen but this is not always the case, which is why it can be helpful to swab the bitch during the earlier part of her season to give you some idea of how it is progressing. Most books on dog breeding will tell you that you must wait for the colour to subside and turn light pink, but in my experience the vast majority of Bulldog bitches are still showing dark colour, sometimes in copious amounts, at the time they are ready to accept the dog.

We have found that by far the best guide as to whether or not a bitch is ready for mating is her willingness to stand. This is a term used to describe a bitch's action if she is touched lightly around the area of the vulva. During a natural mating the bitch will lift her vulva up toward the base of her tail in order to allow the male to penetrate. Of course if she will not do this it makes copulation almost impossible. It is this action which is a strong indicator that the bitch is ready. It must be remembered that not every bitch will behave in the same way, and we have had bitches that would stand from the second or third day of their season and then carry on standing for the next ten to fifteen days.

These indications should only be used as a guide and, generally speaking, most bitches are mated for the first time around the tenth day of their season and again forty-eight hours later. In some cases we do mate the bitch more often than this but there would have to be a good reason – either she has a history of missing and is probably not being caught on the right day or, if she shows a strong desire to stand for the dog, this indicates that possibly the first mating was a little early. The number of matings is of course at the discretion of the stud dog owner. Please remember that it is most important to contact the stud owner immediately your bitch shows colour, as most stud owners will not accept two bitches to their dog over the same period. Once he is booked you can be fairly sure of his availability.

STUD FEES AND BREEDING TERMS

This is an area which can cause much confusion and, in a great many instances, unnecessary bad feeling, simply because the arrangements were not properly written out in the first instance.

Terms relating to stud fees should be explained to you when you first contact the stud dog owner and if they are not, then ask what the dog's terms are before you commit yourself. Some dogs will be available for a set amount, others for a puppy in lieu of a stud fee, but whichever applies, make sure that you are happy with the terms before booking the dog.

Another subject which seems to cause confusion is that of the repeat mating. Generally this term refers to a free mating given by the stud dog to bitches who miss after coming to stud for a fee. It should be remembered that when you pay a stud fee you are paying for a mating, not for puppies, and whether or not the stud dog owner gives a repeat mating is his prerogative. Although it may be generally accepted as correct to do so there is no obligation, and this is something else which should be sorted out when booking the dog.

Breeding terms on bitches are something that we have definitely shied away from. With a breed which can be so difficult to produce puppies from as the Bulldog, terms are very often easier to agree than they are to fulfil. Mostly, breeding terms accompany puppies sold at a reduced price with an agreement that when the bitch has a litter, an agreed number of puppies will be returned to the breeder. Please weigh up the pros and cons before agreeing to breeding terms as, once accepted, it would be quite wrong to try to renege on them at a later date.

If you do decide to go ahead with breeding terms on the bitch, in the interest of all concerned make sure that an agreement is written out, stating how many puppies are to be returned, whether they are to be dogs or bitches, who will have the pick of the litter, whose choice of stud dog it will be, and who pays the stud fee. Both parties should sign and date the document and retain a copy. It is easy to forget the finer points of an agreement over a passage of time, and having it clearly written out can save a lot of bad feeling when the time comes to fulfil the terms.

Chapter Ten

WHELPING

THE PREGNANT BITCH

Assuming that your bitch's visit to the stud dog went well, you now have the seemingly never-ending wait until the time comes to ascertain whether or not she is in whelp. A question often asked is whether there are any special precautions that need to be taken during the early stages of gestation. Basically it will not be necessary to change her old routine until much further into the pregnancy, but do try to avoid letting mated bitches run loose with the other dogs for a few days after they have been to stud. Although it may not be necessary, it certainly cannot do any harm to keep them quiet for a day or two. Remember also that it is possible for a bitch to be mated by another dog right up until the end of her season and she must be kept safely away from the advances of any male admirers. The fact that she has already been mated will make no difference whatsoever and a dual conception is not only possible but has occurred on many occasions.

As I usually have a rough idea of when our bitches are due in season I make sure that any booster inoculations which may be due are carried out before the start of the season.

Worming is carried out on a regular basis throughout the whole kennel but I do try to worm bitches just prior to their coming into season. If this has not been possible, your vet will be able to prescribe a wormer which is safe to use during pregnancy; he will also tell you at what stage of the pregnancy it is safe to worm. Research shows that the effect of worms transmitted from mother to puppies can be the cause of many harmful conditions and can even result in the death of pups in certain cases. For this reason, dosing with a veterinary-prescribed wormer just prior to or during pregnancy is essential.

A common mistake is to increase the food intake of a mated bitch too early in the pregnancy. If the diet she is having is a balanced one and appears to be keeping her in good condition, there really is no reason to change from this until much later on.

It is an unfortunate fact that many bitches will go through the various phases of a pregnancy, following a season, whether in whelp or not and it is not at all uncommon for a mated bitch to suddenly acquire an increased appetite as though eating for a family. A big mistake, but one easily made, is to step up the food and, as she begins to put on weight, become convinced that she is in whelp.

Following a season a bitch will often show signs of a change in character even if not mated, and the incidence of phantom pregnancy in Bulldogs is by no means small. On the other hand, the term 'false pregnancy' is used most commonly when referring to a bitch that has been mated but, having failed to conceive, is still behaving as though in whelp, even producing milk around the time that she would have given birth. This can sometimes make the detection of a definite pregnancy very difficult.

In recent years a blood test has been developed which can tell to a high degree of accuracy whether or not puppies are present. The other option, the one I prefer, is ultra-sound scanning, but not all veterinary practices have the necessary equipment, as a scanner is a very expensive piece of machinery. One of the advantages of scanning as opposed to blood testing is that the scan, although not always accurate, can often give some idea of numbers and can usually detect the difference between a single pup and several puppies, which can be most helpful when the time to whelp comes around.

Normal exercise should be maintained during the pregnancy, but by the sixth week or so, as the bitch begins to show signs of development, especially if carrying a large litter, it would be wiser to start exercising her only on the lead and shortening the walks if she seems to tire before the end. By the eighth week, limit the exercise to a stroll around the garden; but every bitch is different and some like to take a short walk each day almost up until the time they whelp.

For the last week or two, if she is large, it is better to feed two or three small meals a day rather than one large one.

PREPARING THE WHELPING PLACE

Once you have established that your bitch is in whelp the next stage is to decide where she is to have her puppies. As few can afford the luxury of a puppy room, a suitable location will have to be found, preferably where she will not be disturbed more than is absolutely necessary but with access to the garden.

When the location has been decided upon it is a good idea to put the whelping box in position, giving the bitch an opportunity to explore what is to become her new accommodation in a week or two's time. The design of the whelping box which follows is one I have used for many years and have found to be the most easily manageable.

The overall size of the box is three foot six inches by two foot, with a one foot four inch high back and sides. The front is left open but there is a piece of wood three foot six inches by four inches which is fitted across the front of the box for the first few weeks to stop the puppies falling out. This is taken away as soon as the puppies are up on their feet, as they will leave the box to relieve themselves at a surprisingly early age.

It is also most helpful to have a so-called 'pig rail' fitted around the box. This prevents the bitch from trapping a puppy against the wall of the box and is a safe haven between feeds. The rail is made of four inch by one-and-a-half inch timber and is screwed to the three sides of the box approximately four inches from the floor. This provides the puppies with an area four inches wide around the edge of the box in which to rest safely.

Over the years I have found that the best heat source for a bitch with puppies is an infra-red lamp suspended over the whelping box. Use the red bulbs, as the white are far too bright, but be sure to check when buying as some shops refer to the white bulbs as infra-reds. It is also possible to purchase a dull emitter which does not give off any light, only heat, but we have found that, to produce enough heat to reach the puppies, the unit has to be hung so near to the pups the bitch can easily touch the heater, which can get extremely hot. The heat rays from the infra-red bulbs are far more powerful, thus enabling them to be suspended well out of harm's way. The other advantage with the light bulb is that it gives you the opportunity to keep an eye on the puppies without continually disturbing the bitch by switching the room light on and off. The red light does not seem to disturb the bitch at all.

Another piece of equipment I have found to be indispensable when whelping a bitch is a small heated pad, obtainable from most good chemists. These pads are like small electric blankets and have the same heat control, usually with three settings. One of them, covered with a towel and placed in a cardboard box, makes an ideal incubator for new-born puppies whether between births, in the case of a self-whelped litter, or in the case of delivery by caesarean section, after your return from the vet's while the bitch comes around from the anaesthetic. We normally keep the blanket on its highest setting for new-born puppies, but they will not settle if uncomfortable and will attempt to find a cooler part of the box. If new-born puppies are noisy there is generally something amiss.

THE START OF LABOUR

From one week before the bitch is due to whelp, start taking her temperature twice daily. Digital thermometers are ideal, as the reading is clear and extremely accurate. If possible try to get one which measures in Fahrenheit, as this is the scale used by most dog people. If you ring someone for advice the chances are that they will ask you what her temperature is in Fahrenheit.

Although the readings will vary slightly depending on factors such as the time of day, it will generally be found that the body temperature will be around 100-101F. Keep a record of the bitch's temperature each day so that a change will be immediately detected.

Often one of the first signs of a bitch coming into labour will be her reluctance to eat, but this is not always the case. Some bitches are prepared to eat even when labour is well advanced, although I would never allow it at this stage. Around whelping time, approximately sixty-three days after mating, one would normally expect to see a drop in temperature to around 98.4F. Often at this stage the bitch will start to tremble and look a little anxious. These are the earliest indications that she is in the first stages of labour.

The problem with using the temperature as a guide is that some bitches stay at a significantly low temperature for some time, making detection easy, whereas others drop and start to come up again so quickly that you may well miss the lowest point.

When the temperature has returned to normal, around the 100F mark, you will generally find that the bitch will start to pant and scratch up her bedding. This is the stage of the labour that can be the most tiring and nerve-wracking for both bitch and owner, and it is when I would normally telephone our vet to tell him that we definitely have a bitch in the early stages of labour and get confirmation that someone will be available during the next twenty-four hours should assistance be required.

There is no hard and fast rule regarding the duration of this stage of labour, but under no circumstances leave a bitch unattended once this phase has been reached. The chances are that the panting will go on for a long time, sometimes as much as twenty-four hours.

Most bitches like to have a thick layer of newspaper in their whelping box at this time to dig into, as this 'nest building' action seems to help bring on the next stage of labour, the contractions.

THE SECOND STAGE

You may well find that about now the bitch will start to vomit a white froth with the appearance of whipped egg-white. This is caused by the excessive panting which has turned saliva into froth which she has swallowed and then in turn vomits. Although quite normal during a Bulldog whelping, it can still be quite worrying. Restrict the bitch's intake of fluids at this stage and certainly do not tempt her to drink by offering milk or other such liquid; just a very occasional lap of water is all that she will require. If things do not go according to plan and she needs to have a caesarean section, it will be far safer to anaesthetise her on an empty stomach.

After the bitch has been panting for some time, often going right through the night, you will notice that every so often she will stop, almost as though she is listening to something. This is the first indication that her contractions have started and over the next couple of hours you should start to see signs that she is pushing and these contractions will get steadily stronger.

One of the most difficult questions to answer is how long should she be allowed to push before contacting the vet. The main problem here is that you cannot expect the bitch to produce a puppy until the contractions have become strong enough and when they are pushing at full strength most bitches put a terrific effort into it. If the contractions do not seem to strengthen and are only half-hearted after several hours, it would be a good idea to have a word with your vet, just in case the bitch is suffering with uterine inertia and will not progress to a stage where she can deliver her own puppies.

If this is not the case and she seems to be pushing well, we would normally wait for one hour and then, if there is still no sign of a puppy, contact the vet.

THE BIRTH

The first sign of a puppy will be the appearance of the water bag at the opening of the vulva, assuming that the amnion, the fluid-filled bag containing the puppy, is intact. Otherwise, depending on whether the puppy is coming head first (anterior presentation) or tail first (posterior or breech presentation), you may well see a foot or, better still, a pair of feet appear.

A puppy out of the water bag may be more difficult for the bitch to pass and it is useful to have a piece of towelling handy to help get a grip on the puppy to assist in its delivery. Remember only to pull when the bitch is contracting and pull down towards the bitch's feet.

If the puppy has arrived in the amnion sack, this should be torn open as quickly as possible; we have found very few Bulldog bitches attempt to do this. Clear any membrane away from the puppy's face by wiping it with a piece of towelling. It is most important, as soon as the puppy has arrived, to make sure that the airways are clear. Hold the puppy's head down to drain any fluid from the lungs and, at the same time, rub the puppy quite vigorously to stimulate it and encourage those first gasps of breath.

If the puppy does not seem to be breathing it is worth spending time working on the problem, as it can sometimes be several minutes before you detect any sign of life. If the difficulty seems to be that the lungs are full of fluid and mucus is coming from the puppy's nose, try shaking the puppy in a downward motion: this will help to remove liquid from the lungs and generally help to clear the airways.

If the puppy arrives out of the water bag, see whether or not the afterbirth is attached. If it is not, then make a note of this, as the vet will want to know how many have been retained. I do not allow our bitches to eat their afterbirths.

If the puppy is still attached to its afterbirth, it should be separated by holding the umbilical cord with a finger and thumb about one inch away from the puppy's tummy. Make sure that you do not pull on the cord and risk giving the puppy a hernia. With the other hand separate the afterbirth from the cord with a ripping action using a finger nail, ensuring that you do not pull on the part of the cord leading to the puppy. It is this tearing action, similar to the bitch chewing through the cord, which seals off the blood supply. If you were to cut through the cord with scissors the puppy would probably bleed to death. If there is bleeding from the cord after it has been separated from the afterbirth, try pinching the end of the cord between a finger and nail; this will often seal it. If this is not effective, the only alternative is to tie the cord with a fairly strong thread approximately three-quarters of an inch from the puppy's stomach.

Many books recommend tying the cord with a strong thread as a matter of course before detaching the afterbirth, but this can cause a problem when the puppies are returned to their mother, as most bitches will not tolerate anything foreign attached to their pups and will lick and lick until it has been removed.

It is most important not to let newly-born puppies become chilled, and plenty of warm, dry towels will be needed during the whelping.The puppy, after being thoroughly dried, can be placed in the cardboard box, on the heated pad, out of harm's way, while you await the arrival of the next puppy. It will sometimes be found that putting puppies on the bitch to suckle between births will actually stimulate contractions.

To be prepared for every eventuality, it is a good idea to have a small cardboard box containing a hot-water bottle and some clean towels ready, just in case you have to take the bitch to the vet for a caesarean section. This will enable you to return home with the puppies in a warm environment.

Bulldog mothers can be rather clumsy, although this does not apply to all of them by any means. It is a sad fact, though, that each year many puppies are lost due to suffocation when left unsupervised with their mothers for even a short space of time. Because of the sheer heft of bulldog bitches it is difficult to manoeuvre around the confines of a whelping box, and puppies left unattended may well be either lain, sat or trodden on. For this reason the rearing of bulldog puppies is a time-consuming business and the litter will need constant monitoring for the first few weeks if no losses are to be suffered.

AFTER-CARE

When we are sure that the whelping is over and the bitch is settled with her puppies, we usually offer her a drink of water and a light meal. For the first twenty-four hours we give the bitch light meals of chicken or boiled fish and the following day start to resume normal feeding. If she has a large litter she will need all of the sustenance she can get and it is important to remember that to produce plenty of milk she will need to take in plenty of liquids. The occasional drink of the same powdered milk used for fostering puppies is ideal. It is always a good idea to have a can of this in stock if you have a bitch due to whelp, just in case her milk is slow coming through and the puppies can be supplemented for a feed or two. For this purpose a baby's feeding bottle is most suitable.

It is important to make sure that each puppy is feeding from the bitch. It is sometimes difficult to tell whether a puppy is actually feeding or just appearing to suckle. Some bulldog puppies need encouraging to get a proper hold of the teat. Those who have not mastered the act of suckling will soon start to show signs of losing condition.

Even if you have been lucky enough to have a self-whelped litter, still ask the vet to come out and check the bitch over. Some like to give a multi-vitamin injection, and if not all of the afterbirths were passed, an injection will be given to speed their ejection before they can start to cause problems. Your vet may also prescribe a course of antibiotics.

While the vet is checking the bitch over ask for a check on the puppies as well to see if any have a cleft pallet, a condition occasionally seen in the breed, where the roof of the mouth has not completely formed. If you have been unlucky and one or more of the puppies is found to have this condition, it is far better to ask your vet to put the affected puppies to sleep than to be tempted to keep them, as not only will they eventually die but in the process, as they grow weaker, they will unsettle the bitch and we have heard of several healthy puppies being laid or stood on by a bitch frantically trying to placate a cleft puppy which is unable to feed. You must be practical for the sake of the rest of the litter.

Bulldogs are a breed unlike any other and certain conditions occur with them that are rarely, if ever, encountered in other dogs and therefore seldom seen by the veterinary profession. One such condition is evident in newly-born puppies, affecting their hind feet, giving the appearance that they have been born deformed. The hind feet can almost turn back on themselves and, when the puppy is lying on the floor, they stick up in the air, almost like flippers. Although it is not known what causes puppies to be born with feet so formed, it is a fault which will correct itself within the first two or three weeks. Although we must have seen literally dozens of these puppies over the years, we have never known one not to grow out of it and with no lasting side-effects. It can be a surprise when first seen and many bullpups have been put to sleep on the assumption that they will be deformed for life.

Another condition, affecting newly-whelped bitches in particular, is that of head-shaking, usually within a day or two of whelping. Often when the bitches are lying out with their puppies they will start to nod or shake their head, sometimes quite vigorously. In the early days this was normally diagnosed by our vets as eclampsia, as the symptoms could be similar to the onset of this fairly common, but serious, condition, and an injection of calcium would be given, usually to no effect. It was some years later that I found a vet familiar with the breed who considered the problem to be stress-related. Since then we have observed the condition on many occasions and, with peace and quiet, it seems to pass quite quickly; but of course if the bitch seems to be getting distressed in any way, do not hesitate to get in contact with your vet.

Generally speaking, if veterinary assistance is needed with a newly-whelped bitch, ask the vet to call at the house. It is most unfair to expect a bitch with a newly-whelped litter to accept being dragged off to the vet – apart from the obvious risk of exposing her to infection.

Bulldogs are usually born with front dewclaws and these should be left intact. Dewclaws are not removed in this breed.

Although our bitches normally whelp on newspaper, as soon as the whelping is completed this is changed for the imitation sheepskin-type veterinary bedding. This is not only comfortable for the bitch but provides good traction for the puppies when they start to get around at three weeks or so.

Chapter Eleven

REARING

THE FIRST FEW DAYS

The first few days can be crucial and the first week is probably the most perilous time of a puppy's entire life. As previously mentioned, it is imperative to make sure that new-born puppies are suckling and not just appearing to do so. After rearing several litters it will become much easier to distinguish between a good and a bad feeder, but to give some idea as to how the puppy is feeding, it is a good policy to weigh puppies at birth and each day thereafter, charting their progress.

Bulldogs can be surprisingly large at birth and sixteen-ounce puppies are not that uncommon, although around ten to twelve ounces would be considered an average weight. I have reared puppies weighing as little as six ounces at birth, but puppies this small will require extra attention. It is quite normal for puppies to lose weight immediately after birth and they can in fact take several days before returning to their birth weight. Generally, though, a pattern throughout the litter will begin to emerge. A puppy losing far more weight than the others must be closely watched, and supplemented with a bottle if necessary before becoming to weak to feed at all.

Before putting puppies on to feed for the first time, lightly squeeze one of the bitch's teats to confirm the presence of milk. It will generally be found that the teats toward the rear of the bitch will not only contain the most milk but will also be the easiest from which to extract it. For this reason try to keep these for the smaller puppies, or those which seem to find suckling the most difficult.

The process of a puppy feeding from the mother is basically one of suction and any puppy making a smacking sound whilst feeding is not succeeding in making the tight seal around the teat necessary in order to extract milk. It is very often these noisy feeding puppies which go from one teat to another due to the frustration of not satisfying their hunger.

When a puppy is feeding well, close observation will show a large pink tongue wrapped tightly around the teat while the puppy rhythmically presses on the bitch with the front feet, satisfying the appetite. This is what we all hope for, and watching puppies that are 'good doers' is most rewarding. It will sometimes be the case that a puppy has a preference for a particular teat where the art of suckling has been mastered, and will refuse any other.

A litter of eight puppies, pictured at nine days old. At this stage, the bitch cares for all the puppies' needs, feeding them and cleaning them.

Kingrock Hotpants with her three-week-old litter, sired by her son, Kingrock Benjamin Barnrat. Matings this close are not common, and before attempting to in-breed this closely it is imperative that the breeder has an in-depth knowledge of both pedigrees, and knows what they are likely to produce.

Equally important to the feeding and keeping warm of new-born puppies is making sure that the bitch is cleaning them regularly, as many problems, and not uncommonly death, can result from constipation in young puppies. If it is the bitch's first litter, especially if delivered by caesarean section, she may well be reluctant to clean them for the first day or two, and in some cases never accepts that this is a part of motherhood. To begin with, holding a puppy up to her mouth for her to lick may encourage her to start but, if not, it is imperative that you clean them by hand. A pad of cotton wool dampened in warm water and wiped down the puppy's stomach toward the tail in the same manner as the bitch would lick, will cause the puppy to urinate quite readily and this should be repeated every two or three hours. The puppy will not pass faeces at each cleaning but, probably, every second or third time and, providing that when this happens the motion is not hard or crumbly, indicating constipation, there is no need to worry.

Many breeders prefer to keep the puppies away from the bitch in their heated box and just return them to her every two hours to be fed. If this is the method you have decided on, making sure that the puppies are cleaned is particularly important as the bitch will have very little opportunity to see to them herself, although in our experience this is not something which worries the bitches unduly.

Much will depend on the bitch herself as some have far greater maternal instincts than others. Generally we have found that our bitches will accept this method but most will soon let you know if you are late putting the puppies on to feed. These two-hourly feeds, night and day, will need to be maintained for the first ten days or so, depending on the size of the puppies. After this age, normally only feed every three hours through the night, but continue with the two-hourly feeds through the day.

If you are rearing a litter in this way, always put the puppies in another room far enough away so that the mother cannot hear them. If this is not possible, leave a radio on in the room in an attempt to avoid the bitch hearing her puppies. Most bitches will settle between feeds quite happily providing that they cannot hear their pups. If she will not settle without them, there really is no option but to return them to her and resort to keeping twenty four-hour surveillance on the litter.

Most puppies will have loose motions for the first few days and it is most important to keep a check on the puppies' bottoms, ensuring that they do not become blocked with dried faeces. This can be a problem, particularly with puppies with screw tails which cover the anus and can easily stop the puppy from passing a motion. If this does happen, put a dab of vaseline on to the area. This will normally soften the faeces sufficiently to allow them to be gently removed and re-applying vaseline each day will usually stop the problem from recurring.

It is more comfortable for the bitch if you keep the puppies' nails from growing too long. Trimming them at about two weeks and then every two weeks or so afterwards will help prevent the bitch becoming sore around the teats.

If the litter was delivered by caesarean, particular attention should be given to the area of incision. If the operation was carried out on the flank, all that will be required is to keep an eye on the wound, ensuring it is kept clean and is repairing with no sign of discharge. Your vet will have asked you to take her back for him to see in ten days in order to remove the sutures. If the incision was mid-line (down the middle of the body between the mammaries), it is important to make sure that the area does not become sore, as very little air can get to this area and it can become very damp. Each day gently wipe the area with a clean damp cloth, then carefully pat dry, and finish by sprinkling a little baby talcum powder over the area to stop heat rash from occurring.

WEANING

Unless the bitch is producing insufficient milk the need to wean will depend greatly on the size of the litter. If she is rearing a large litter it is only fair to start helping out as soon as

ABOVE: Three nine-week-old puppies sired by Ch. Kingrock Captain Christian. The pup on the left went on to become Swed. Nor. Ch. Kingrock Tudor Flower, and the pup on the right went on to become Nor. Ch. Kingrock Union Jack.

RIGHT: A litter of Kingrock puppies pictured at eight weeks.

possible, although under normal circumstances this would not be before three weeks of age.

I always wean puppies on to scraped beef. This is obtained by running a sharp knife over a piece of lean top-quality beef: the resulting paste is ideal to encourage the puppies off their mother's milk diet. As well as being extremely palatable, scraped beef is also easily digestible as opposed to mince, which may be rather too heavy a meal.

With a litter being weaned at three weeks, continue to feed the scraped beef two or three times a day for a week or so. If the litter is not large, say three or four puppies, and the bitch appears to have plenty of milk, do not be in too much of a hurry to wean, as the longer they can be left on the mother the easier it will be when the time does come to wean, but in any event by five weeks of age weaning should be well under way.

As the puppies grow, so their appetite for solid food will grow with them and if you were not to find some alternative, most of your time would be spent scraping beef! There are some extremely good complete foods on the market which have been specially designed for young puppies and are most suitable. These foods are normally referred to as 'expanded', and come in the form of small pellets of ground food. Do not use the complete foods which have flakes resembling cornflakes, as these foods are most unsuitable for weaning bulldog puppies.

The expanded food pellets should be soaked in cold water for several hours before they are required, as they take quite some time to soften through to the centre, which is essential before being mixed with beef and fed. By this stage it is acceptable to use finely minced or, better still, ground beef as a replacement to the scraped, but it must still be of exceptional quality, and under no circumstances use pet mince.

This mixture of meal and mince can be used as an alternate to a feed from the bitch. Gradually increase the quantity, thereby lessening her work load. When the bitch starts significantly to decrease her feeding, it will become necessary to begin offering the puppies liquid feeds as well. In the early stages we find that many puppies find it rather difficult to get the hang of lapping and, as a consequence, much of the milk feed ends up being blown back down their noses. This is not something that I like to see young puppies do, as it can easily get drawn down on to the lungs and may even cause pneumonia.

To avoid this risk rely once more on the expanded food, again soaked in cold water until of a consistency which will mash easily with a fork. To this add one of the proprietary puppy milk mixes made up as recommended on the can. Most good pet shops and chemists, and some vets, keep it in stock.

At between five and six weeks the puppies should be almost totally independent of their mother and at this age you will normally be feeding them five or six times a day.

It is far better for the puppies to have a little and often, rather than over-taxing the system with two or three large meals, which will often cause digestive problems resulting in diarrhoea. By nine or ten weeks the feeds can be reduced to four meals a day.

COLOUR AND REGISTRATION

Colour in puppies is not always an easy thing to establish. Most reds are born almost black in colour, lightening within the first few weeks. Fawns again can be most deceptive and it is not always possible to distinguish between red and fawn until several weeks old. Brindle puppies do not always show stripes from birth, but after a day or two will usually start to show signs of brindling around the head area and on the legs. Do not be in too much of a hurry to register puppies; if you are not sure of their colours it is better to wait a week or two than to register them incorrectly.

WORMING

The importance of keeping puppies regularly wormed cannot be overstated. Worm at three weeks of age, again at six and once more at nine weeks. If the puppy will be in a new home when due for the third worming, the new owners should be advised of the date for this and given instructions as to the brand and where it can be obtained. We prefer to buy worming preparations from the vet. Although perhaps a little more expensive than some obtainable over the counter, the resulting effect is usually far better: when dealing with something which can affect a puppy's wellbeing to the extent that worming can, it is not wise to become overly economical.

EYE COLOUR

Eye colour is another subject which seems to cause concern during those early weeks. Puppies' eyes are naturally blue when they first open at around ten days and this will change over the following few weeks to a dark brown and hopefully will end up very dark, almost black. Each year a percentage of puppies are born with truly blue eyes, which is a different thing. Blue-eyed puppies' eyes are china blue and show no sign of darkening with time. They are similar in appearance to the wall eye seen in Old English Sheepdogs and merle-coloured Collies. Blue-eyed puppies have appeared from time to time over the years and are certainly not a new phenomenon.

Although it is disappointing to get this fault, as it will be heavily penalised in the show ring since the standard asks for the eyes to be 'very dark – almost, if not quite, black', it should be borne in mind that, as faults go, it at least has the benefit of not causing the dog any discomfort and can only be considered a serious fault from a cosmetic point of view. Having said that, it is one we could well do without, and to breed from a dog or bitch with this fault is to do future breeders a great disservice.

MOBILITY

Bulldog puppies can be notoriously slow at getting up and around. Ideally, by three weeks of age they should be well on their way to becoming mobile. It is very important to make sure that they are able to get good traction on the floor-covering of their whelping box, and this is most important even with tiny puppies. Newspaper, apart from being uncomfortable for the bitch, is far too smooth a service on which to expect puppies to learn to walk. The sheepskin type of veterinary bedding mentioned earlier, or even blankets, are far more suitable. Every effort should be made and encouragement given to get puppies up and about before they become too heavy. Puppies are usually able to walk, even if only for a short distance, by four weeks of age at the latest. If your litter are showing no signs of doing this, then it would be worth contacting an experienced breeder or the stud dog owner to ask whether they would be prepared to have a look at the litter and advise on the best course of action.

One other point, but a very important one to establish before selling puppy males, is whether or not both testicles are descended. Even if the puppy is being sold purely as a pet, it is still advisable to mention it to the new owners if the puppy is not yet entire. Hopefully, this problem will correct itself within the following week or two, although this is something which no one can guarantee.

Chapter Twelve

THE BULLDOG IN GREAT BRITAIN

So many great dogs and great Bulldoggers have contributed to the breed's development in the UK since the turn of the century that to list them all would be almost an impossibility. For this reason I have concentrated on those involved in the breed over more recent years and a good starting point seemed to be the year which saw The Bulldog Club Inc. start out on its second century, 1975.

Limiting the era covered would not, in itself, sufficiently lower the numbers, so, for this reason, I have concentrated on those kennels which have bred a minimum of three UK champions within the period covered.

All of the dogs and bitches which have produced three or more UK champions since 1975 are mentioned in the following paragraphs.

PAT DELLAR: MERRIVEEN
At about the time of the Bulldog Club's Centenary Show, a kennel which would prove to have a beneficial effect on the breed over the following decades was beginning to evolve in the Hertfordshire countryside. Pat Dellar, owner of the famous Merriveen Boxers during the late fifties and early sixties, and a much respected breeder of pedigree dogs of several breeds had, after some years absence from the world of show dogs, turned her attention to the Bulldog.

Pat felt that she needed a fresh challenge and, having no desire to return to a breed in which she had already met with success, saw the Bulldog as providing just such an opportunity.

At that time the breed had serious health problems, which many of those involved with Bulldogs considered unfortunate but unavoidable, although some kennels were trying their utmost to eradicate such inherent problems as elongated soft palate and entropion from their stock.

Over the following years the Merriveen kennel bred no fewer than eleven UK champions, a record for the breed, and in the process produced such great sires as Ch. Merriveen Happy Daze, the sire of seven UK champions, Ch. Merriveen Halcyon Daze, the sire of five UK champions, and Merriveen Son of Satan, with six UK champion progeny.

Ch. Merriveen Pepsi Cola, owned and bred by Pat Dellar.

Pearce.

Ch. Merriveen Happy Memories, owned and bred by Pat Dellar.

LES AND ELLEN COTTON: ALDRIDGE

The Aldridge kennel of Les and Ellen Cotton has not only produced many champions at home and abroad, but also owned and bred the famous Champion Aldridge Advent Gold, sire of nine UK champions. This breeding can be found in the pedigrees of many of today's winners, and one of Advent Gold's progeny, Ch. Aldridge Avanti, was the sire of four UK champions. Another bred by this kennel, Ch. Aldridge Aristocrat of Brandywell, owned by Bill and Jean Cartwright, was the sire of five UK champions. The kennel also owned and bred one of the only two bitches to have produced three UK champion progeny within the period covered, Aldridge Ardent Arlene.

PAT AND NORMAN DAVIS: OCOBO

This kennel not only bred champions but their dogs sired them as well. Ch. Ocobo Skipper, the first champion to be made up by this kennel, was the sire of three UK champions. His son, Ch. Quintic Amos of Ocobo, bred by Pat Perkins, also made something of a name for himself as a quality stud and sired four UK champions. The other top producing male owned by this kennel was Ch. Storming Passion of Ocobo, bred by Mrs Rich and the sire of four UK champions.

Ch. Sandean Sophies Baby: Current recordholder for the greatest number of CCs won by a Bulldog bitch in the UK.

OTHER FAMOUS KENNELS

Many of the kennels which have bred champions in recent years have had an association with the breed which goes back a long way. Harold and Audie Hayball's **Thydeal** kennel has been associated with champion stock over a period of many years, as has the **Bryneatons** affix of Jean and Godfrey Evans. Then there are Jack and Kath Cook of the **Jackath** kennel, Frank Huxley's **Ellesmere** affix, Les and Dorrie Thorpe's **Tuffnuts**, Ruth Murray's **Brenuth** kennel and Fred and Anne Higginbottom's **Tretun** affix. George and Eva Parker, owners of the famous **'Of the Regions'** affix, were also the owners of Ch. Brumigum Stroller Boy of the Regions, the top producing stud during the period covered, with ten UK champion progeny.

CHRIS THOMAS AND GRAHAM GODFREY: KINGROCK

This is my own prefix and the first litter born at Kingrock was sired by George and Eva Parker's Stroller Boy, out of Chiansline White Regality of Kingrock. From this litter was kept a red and white bitch, Kingrock My-Nora-Tee, who is the only other bitch to have produced three or more UK champion progeny within the period I am discussing.

Ch. Ocobo Tully, owned and bred by Pat Davis.

Sw. Nor. Eng. Ch. Tretun Sam Wella at Kingrock, owned by Chris Thomas and Graham Godfrey, bred by Anne Higginbottom. *Gibbs.*

ABOVE: Ch. Kingrock Canis Pugnax, owned and bred by Chris Thomas.

Pearce.

RIGHT: Ch. Kingrock Star at Ocobo, owned by Pat and Norman Davis, bred by Chris Thomas.

We have had the good fortune consistently to produce champions both at home and abroad since the seventies, and were particularly fortunate to breed and own the prolific sire Ch. Kingrock Freezo, father of seven UK champions.

DENNIS SHAW: DENBROUGH

Another great sire, and the dog CC winner at the Bulldog Club's Centenary Show, was Ch. Beechlyn Golden Nugget of Denbrough, owned by Dennis Shaw and bred by Joe Fox. Nugget was the sire of seven UK champions and many other winning progeny. He was also one of the foundation stones of the Merriveen kennel and subsequently appeared in the pedigrees of most winning lines throughout the seventies and eighties. Nugget won forty-two CCs, a record for the breed.

Dennis Shaw's kennel also produced the notable stud Ch. Denbrough Leander, the sire of five UK champions.

OTHER CHAMPIONS

Another dog to have made an impact in both the show ring and the progeny department is the famous Ch. Willsmere Solid Silver, owned and bred by Viv and Graham Williams. Not only was he the sire of three UK champions but he also won the prestigious 'Bulldog of the Year' award on no fewer than four occasions, a record that will be difficult to break.

In more recent times the well-known kennels of John and Sheila Nattrass, **Bonifacio**, Bill and Sheila Roberts, **Isgraig**, with their prolific homebred stud Ch. Isgraig Red Baron, the sire of four UK champions, and Noel and Ann Morgan, **Ringablock,** owners of Eskaidee Mighty Monarch of Ringablock, the sire of three UK champions, have all made a substantial contribution to the breed.

Wencar Silver Sonlight, owned and bred by Ron and Carol Newman, is one of the only three non-champions to have sired three or more UK champion progeny since 1975. Silver Sonlight was the sire of six UK champions, as was his sire, one of the other non-champions, Merriveen Son of Satan.

These are just some of the people and Bulldogs currently helping to ensure the well-being of our breed in its homeland. Of course there are many more which space does not allow me to mention.

THE BULLDOG OF THE YEAR

In 1977 the Bulldog Club Incorporated launched a competition which was to become one of the highlights of the Bulldoggers' show calendar, The Bulldog of the Year.

The basic format for this competition has remained virtually unchanged from those early days and is proof that the organisers had the foresight to see what the exhibitors wanted, and the event has grown from strength to strength. The interest created both at home and abroad by this unique event ensures a crowded ringside each year, with many parties of Bulldoggers from around the world helping to engender the unique atmosphere which is always present. Entry to the competition is by invitation only and each exhibit must have won at least one Challenge Certificate within the previous twelve months.

The system of judging is quite simple and to be asked to be one of the three championship show judges who officiate each year is an honour indeed. I had the pleasure of judging at this competition in 1989 and it was an unforgettable experience.

The judges examine each of the exhibits, with all three judging at the same time in different positions of the ring and the dogs entering the ring in groups of three, a masterly feat of stewarding. At no stage are the judges allowed to confer and, when all of the dogs of one sex have been judged, cards showing each judge's placings are handed to the show manager. This is then repeated for the bitches.

At the climax of the event the final results are collated and read out in reverse order, starting with Reserve Dog, Reserve Bitch, Best Opposite Sex and Bulldog of the Year. Just these four placings are revealed, as all of the dogs which compete are winners in their own right.

PAST WINNERS

YEAR: 1977
Judges: Claude Bannister, Marjorie Barnard & Arthur Westlake
Bulldog of the Year: CH. BELLUM PREMIER
Breeder: John Driver MRCVS
Owners: John Driver & Wendy Phillips
Sex: B.   Whelped: November 11th 1974
Sire: CH. HARADA BEN PEPPERDINE
Dam: SAUCY SCARLE

1977:
Ch. Bellum Premier.

Garwood.

YEAR: 1978
Judges: Les Lund, Norman Pitts & Jack Cook
Bulldog of the Year: CH. OUTDOORS JUBILANT
Breeder/Owner: Dora Wakefield.
Sex: D   Whelped: August 23rd 1977
Sire: CH. ALDRIDGE ADVENT GOLD
Dam: OUTDOORS SUNSHINE

1978:
Ch. Outdoors Jubilant.

Garwood.

YEAR: 1979
Judges: Marjorie Barnard, Les Thorpe and Ormsby Issard-Davis.
Bulldog of the Year: CH. OUTDOORS JUBI JUNIOR
Breeder/Owner: Dora Wakefield
Sex: D   Whelped: October 13th 1978
Sire: CH. OUTDOORS JUBILANT
Dam: POLLYANNA OF OUTDOORS

YEAR: 1980
Judges: Kath Cook, George Parker & Tom Horner.
Bulldog of the Year: CH. ESKAIDEE BAGGAGE
Breeder/Owner: Margueritte Cook
Sex: B   Whelped: September 4th 1978
Sire: CH. ALDRIDGE ADVENT GOLD
Dam: ESKAIDEE TROLLOP

YEAR: 1981
Judges: Jack Bateman. Godfrey Evans & John Story.
Bulldog of the Year: CH. MERRIVEEN MAYBE BABY handled by her owner Pat Dellar.
(Also in the photograph is journalist Stafford Sommerfield, 2nd from right).
Breeder: Chris Thomas
Owner: Pat Dellar
Sex: B   Whelped: March 6th 1979
Sire: MERRIVEEN SON OF SATAN
Dam: KINGROCK MY-NORA-TEE

1981:
Ch. Merriveen Maybe Baby.

Garwood.

YEAR: 1982
Judges: Jack Cook, George Parker & Norman Pitts.
Bulldog of the Year: CH. WELTOR JACK OF DIAMONDS OF JORONA
Breeders: Peter & Leslie Rothwell
Owners: John & Fiona Rowe
Sex: D   Whelped: June 8th 1981
Sire: CH. BRUMIGUM STROLLER BOY OF THE REGIONS
Dam: JORONA WINTER JASMINE

YEAR: 1983
Judges: Ron Bowers, Les Thorpe & Tom Horner.
Bulldog of the Year: CH. STOCKBULL BIG BEN
Breeder/Owner: Graham Payne
Sex: D   Whelped: January 22nd 1981
Sire: BOWCREST PATTON
Dam: CANDY OF FULHAM

YEAR: 1984
Judges: Dorothy Jones, Ralph Chambers & Norman Pitts.
Bulldog of the Year: CH. TYEGARTH JACOB OF KELLOE
Breeder: Sheila Cartwright
Owners: Chris Bruton & David McHale
Sex: D   Whelped: December 19th 1979
Sire: CH. MERRIVEEN HAPPY DAZE
Dam: TYEGARTH GABRIELLE

YEAR: 1985
Judges: Ada Pitts, Dorrie Thorpe & Harold Hayball.
Bulldog of the Year: CH. MERRIVEEN HALCYON DAZE
Breeder/Owner: Pat Dellar
Sex: D   Whelped: August 20th 1980
Sire: CH. MERRIVEEN HAPPY DAZE
Dam: CH. MERRIVEEN PEPSI COLA

1985:
Ch. Merriveen
Halcyon Daze.

Hartley.

YEAR: 1986
Judges: Jean Evans, Pat Dellar & Godfrey Evans.
Bulldog of the Year: BULLZAYE SANDY McNAB handled by Betty Cassidy
Breeder/Owner: Richard & Betty Cassidy
Sex: D   Whelped: January 1st 1985
Sire: WENCAR SILVER SONLIGHT
Dam: MERRIVEEN JASMINE

1986:
Bullzaye Sandy
McNab.

Hartley.

YEAR: 1987
Judges: Norman Pitts, Anne Higginbottom & Les Cotton
Bulldog of the Year: CH. WILLSMERE SOLID SILVER handled by breeder/owner Viv
Williams
Sex: D   Whelped: May 20th 1986
Sire: CH. ALDRIDGE AVANTI
Dam: CH. WILLSMERE NAUGHTY BUT NICE

Bulldog of the
Year in 1987,
1988, 1991 and
1992: Ch.
Willsmere Solid
Silver.

Hartley.

YEAR: 1988
Judges: George Parker, George Walsh & John Davies.
Bulldog of the Year: CH. WILLSMERE SOLID SILVER

YEAR: 1989
Judges: Vera May, Chris Thomas & Minnie Wearmouth,
Bulldog of the Year: CH. STORMING PASSION OF OCOBO
Breeder: Mrs Rich
Owners: Norman & Pat Davis
Sex: D   Whelped: March 26th 1988
Sire: CH. QUINTIC AMOS OF OCOBO
Dam: BELIRE SKIP 'N HOP

1989:
Ch. Storming
Passion of Ocobo.

Hartley.

YEAR: 1990
Judges: Carol Newman, John Story & Tom Horner.
Bulldog of the Year: CH. AUDSTAN SVENGALI
Breeder/Owner: Nina Boulton
Sex: D   Whelped: July 25th 1986
Sire: CH. ALDRIDGE AVANTI
Dam: WALLBREN LITTLE PRETENDER

YEAR: 1991
Judges: Gwen Biddle, Bob Wain & Ann van den Heuvel,
Bulldog of the Year: CH. WILLSMERE SOLID SILVER

YEAR: 1992
Judges: Marge Spickernell, Ada Pitts & Arthur Rowe.
Bulldog of the Year: CH. WILLSMERE SOLID SILVER

YEAR: 1993
Judges: Jim Adams, Les Thorpe & Pat Perkins
Bulldog of the Year: CH. BRAMPTON RED JOSHUA handled by Terry Davison
Breeders/Owners: Terry & Angela Davison
Sex: D   Whelped: November 3rd 1989
Sire: CH. ISGRAIG RED BARON
Dam: BRAMPTON SUGAR GIRL

1993:
Ch. Red Joshua.

Hartley.

YEAR: 1994
Judges: Bob Haydock, Dorrie Thorpe and Noel Morgan.
Bulldog of the Year: CH. OCOBO TULLY, handled by Kevin Davis
Owner/breeder: Pat Davis
Sex: D   Whelped: October 25th 1992
Sire: BEWLEY ANZAC
Dam: OCOBO NEW EDITION

1994:
Ch. Ocobo Tully.

Hartley.

Chapter Thirteen

THE BULLDOG IN NORTH AMERICA

THE HISTORY OF THE BULLDOG CLUB OF AMERICA

Prior to 1890 no breed club existed for Bulldogs in the USA. Mr H.D. Kendall of Lowell, Massachusetts, organised a meeting of Bulldog enthusiasts at the Mechanics Hall, Boston, on April 1st 1890. The Bulldog Club of America grew from this.

Although the English Standard was adopted by the newly-formed club, it was revised by BCA committee members in 1896 and has remained unchanged, with the exception of the rule disqualifying Dudley noses, included in 1914, to this day.

The famous Charles G. Hopton, owner of the Rodney affix. In 1893 he imported Reve-Royal, Cameron and Lady Monarch from the UK.

ABOVE: Charles Hopton judging Bulldogs in 1907.

LEFT: English and Am. Ch. Cefnmabley Queen: Imported from the UK in the late 1930s, she was the top winning bitch at the Chicago Specialty in 1941.

The BCA was recognised by the AKC as the parent club for all Bulldog specialty clubs and in 1950 was reorganised to represent truly the whole of the country. It was then divided into seven divisions, an eighth following later due to a split in one of the divisions. They are democratically run, each division being directed by a separate Board of Governors.

The BCA held its first Specialty show in conjunction with the Westchester KC on February 24th 1891. Later that year, at the Westminster show, the BCA backed an entry of fifty-one Bulldogs with the provision of sixteen cups, medals and cash prizes.

In 1898 the BCA held its first independent show at the Logorot Garden, New York, with an entry of fifty-nine Bulldogs, and the breed drew the second highest entry at the Westminster show of 1910, with two hundred and three entries.

In 1913 the UK import, A.H. Stewart19s Ch. Strathway Prince Albert, won BIS at the prestigious Westminster show. Many other imports, far too numerous to mention, have played a significant part in the development of the breed in the US, complementing the strong bloodlines which already existed. The highlight of the American Bulldoggers calendar must be the BCA National Specialty. Although it is not possible to list all of the winners from the earliest days, I have listed the BoBs since 1980:

Year: 1980   Date: June 1st   Location: Long Beach, CA.
Judge: Marilyn Dundas
Best of Breed: CH. MARSHALL'S MITEY KW
Breeder: Harriet & Roger Marshall
Owner: Harriet & Roger Marshall
Sex: D   Whelped: April 5th 1978   Finished Date: August 25th 1979
Sire: CH. MARINEBULL'S ALL THE WAY
Dam: CH. BAYSIDE DAPHNE

Year: 1981   Date: November 26th   Location: Memphis, TN.
Judge: Phil Schneider
Best of Breed: CH. LORD TIMOTHY SCOTT
Breeder: David Douglas
Owner: Robert Scott & Jerry Watson
Sex: D   Whelped: October 7th 1976   Finished Date: March 20th 1980
Sire: CH. E-LYNN'S BIG JOHN'S THUNDER
Dam: AMIGA DE PERFECTA PRODUCCION

Year: 1982   Date: November 12th   Location: Irving, TX.
Judge: C. D. Richardson
Best of Breed: CH. LODEL'S HIGHJACKER OF KRALAN
Breeder: Jack Krahn & Lois Shrout
Owner: Jack Krahn & Lois Shrout
Sex: D   Whelped: August 14th 1978   Finished Date: April 19th 1980
Sire: CH. DOMINO'S DYNAMO OF GRABEL
Dam: CH. KRALAN'S GYPSY ROSE

Year: 1983   Date: April 9th   Location: Newark, NJ.
Judge: Alfred M. Freedman
Best of Breed: CH. TACKAWANNA GORGEOUS GEORGE
Breeder: Harold & Peggy Willis
Owner: Adelaide & Harold Willis
Sex: D   Whelped: July 16th 1980   Finished Date: June 26th 1981
Sire: CH. DEY-DEL'S DYNAMIC ZEUS
Dam: TACKAWANNA SANDY KLAWS

Year: 1984   Date: September 8th   Location: Portland, OR.
Judge: Beryl Gould
Best of Breed: CH. CHEROKEE YANCEY
Breeder: Cody & June Sickle
Owner: Cody & June Sickle
Sex: D   Whelped: May 31st 1982   Finished Date: May 28th 1983
Sire: CH. CHEROKEE IVANHOE
Dam: CH. CHEROKEE PRIDE

Year: 1985   Date: November 1st   Location: Merrillville, IL.
Judge: Carolyn Ragan
Best of Breed: CH. CHEROKEE YANCEY

Year: 1986   Date: November 28th   Location: Kansas City, MO.
Judge: Jeanne Zalud
Best of Breed: CH. BOWAG'S PO-LAR
Breeder: William Hinkes, Beverly & O'Neill Wagner
Owner: Beverly & O'Neill Wagner
Sex: B   Whelped: March 3rd 1985   Finished Date: Dec. 6th 1985
Sire: CH. BOWAG'S ARTHUR DE DAY
Dam: CH. BOWAG'S BEBE RUBY DAY

Year: 1987   Date: October 30th   Location: San Jose, CA.
Judge: Dorothy Thomas
Best of Breed: CH. KERRS' WINSTON PRIDE O'TUGBOAT
Breeder: Darlene & John Carlin
Owner: Lenora & Robert Kerr & Jonda Zeller
Sex: D   Whelped: October 16th 1986   Finished Date: Aug. 23rd 1987
Sire: NOELEAN LOVER BOY
Dam: CARLIN'S TUGBOAT DUCHESS ANNE

Year: 1988   Date: November 25th   Location: Charlotte, NC.
Judge: Bertha Newbill
Best of Breed: CH. HETHERBULL BOUNTY'S FRIGATE

Breeder: Roberta Arnold
Owner: Jean & Robert Hetherington
Sex: D   Whelped: February 2nd 1987   Finished Date: Sept. 25th 1987
Sire: CH. FREDLYNS BE AY
Dam: BOUNTY'S COMPASS ROSE

Year: 1989   Date: November 24th   Location: Houston, TX.
Judge: Callan S. Riggs
Best of Breed: CH. POWERBULL'S BOOMER ESIASON
Breeder: Brynda Cox, Dan & Toni Powers
Owner: Robert Jensen, Dan & Toni Powers
Sex: D   Whelped: March 14th 1986   Finished Date: Jan. 4th 1987
Sire: CH. POWERBULL'S HOG HANNER
Dam: MARINEBULL'S YES SHE IS II

Year: 1990   Date: November 23rd   Location: Atlanta, GA.
Judge: Cyril Bernfeld
Best of Breed: CH. BRUMAR'S CALL ME HIGGINS
Breeder: Bruce & Mary Jo Armiger
Owner: Sigrid J. Treat
Sex: D   Whelped: July 22nd 1988   Finished Date: Dec. 2nd 1989
Sire: CH. BOWAG'S ROCKY BEAUTY
Dam: BRUMAR'S OUR GAL SOW

Year: 1991 Date: Sept. 13th   Location: Seattle, WA.
Judge: Ernest Hubbard
Best of Breed: CH. TSAR'S FAT MAN'S FINALE
Breeder: David & Bonnie Boucher
Owner: James & Soya Cardello
Sex: D   Whelped: October 27th 1989   Finished Date: Oct. 13th 1990
Sire: CH. TSAR'S CALL ME THE FAT MAN
Dam: BONNIE'S BIG BAD BERTHA

Year: 1992   Date: November 6th   Location: Cromwell, CT.
Judge: John Little
Best of Breed: CH. GLYNDEBOURNE BARITONE
Breeder: Kay Eckels, Fred Harrington & Claire Pettegrew-Tomlinson
Owner: John & Patricia Garrity & Claire Pettegrew-Tomlinson
Sex: D   Whelped: April 29th 1988   Finished Date: July 15th 1989
Sire: CH. SATUIT FRISKY BUSINESS
Dam: GLYNDEBOURNE BRASS FLOURISH

Year: 1993   Date: November 26th   Location: St. Louis, MO.

Judge: Saul D. Schor
Best of Breed: CH. WARMVALLEY GILLIE'S SOPHIA
Breeder: Jane Paul, Madeline Shea & Diane Wallwork
Owner: Madeline Shea & Diane Wallwork
Sex: B   Whelped: March 24th 1989   Finished Date: Nov. 30th 1991
Sire: CH. CHARJO GULLIBULL GILBERT
Dam: CH. BULLSEYE'S PLUM PUDDN'

BULLDOG BREEDERS

SMASHER
OWNED BY KARL FOERSTER, RAY KNUDSON AND RUTH WOODS.

Karl Foerster and Ray Knudson obtained their first Bulldog, Ch. Smasher Josephine, in 1972. This bitch, sired by Mrs A.R. Glass's Ch. Sequel's Smasherjoe, was to form the foundation of today's well-known kennel. In 1991 the kennel joined forces with Ruth Woods, which helped to perpetuate and expand the Smasher breeding programme.

This kennel has produced many winners from its rigid line-breeding, one of the most famous being Ch. Smasher's Al Capp, owned jointly with Carolyn Whiteside. 'Abner', as he is known to his friends, is the product of five generations of in-line breeding and was the No.1 Bulldog in the US in 1987. Having won BOS at the Bulldog Club of America National Specialty show and an All-Breed BIS, he was retired from the show ring at the end of that year. In 1990 he was inducted into the BCA Hall of Fame as a producer of champions, and his portrait hangs in the BCA Gallery of National winners.

Am. Ch. Smasher's Al Capp.

Booth.

Am. Ch. Mardel Fidelis Bianca.

Am. Ch. Mardel Fidelis Banshee.   Kernan.

American. Ch. Fidedlis Darlin Mary Poppins.

Ashbey.

SEMPER FIDELIS
OWNED BY BOB AND SUSAN RODENSKI

One of this Virginia-based kennel's most famous dogs is Mary Poppins, who started her career at six months old at the BCA National weekend, winning reserve Winners Bitch and Best Puppy for the Division V11 Day. In 1992 at the BCA National Day, she was awarded Brood Bitch for the year. Mary Poppins is by Ch. Lebo's Horsefeathers out of Ch. Mardel Fidelis Bianca.

Another notable Bulldog from this kennel is Ch. Mardel Fidelis Banshee, who finished her championship with a BoB (5pt major) at the Piedmont North Carolina BC Specialty. Banshee had seven BoBs and two BOS over numerous other champions before she became a champion. She is by Ch. Cherokee Yancey out of Cherokee Mardel's Fantasia. Mary Poppins' daughter, Ch. Fidelis Kiss Me Kate (Katie), finished her championship at the 1992 BCA National Day, taking Winners Bitch (5pt major). She has numerous Specialty wins. Another Fidelis champion, Ch. Mardel Fidelis Bianca, started her career by taking a 4pt major and Best of Winners at the Division V11 Specialty in North Carolina. She also took BOS at the Westminster KC show in New York City. At the 1993 BCA national weekend she retired, taking Veterans Bitch both days she was entered. In 1994 she will be inducted into the Hall of Fame. Bianca is by Ch. Cherokee Yancey ex Cherokee Mardel's Fantasia.

HOOGH'S
OWNED BY BRUCE AND MINDY SMITH

Based in Massachusetts, the Hoogh's kennel has produced many top-quality Bulldogs. Ch. Hoogh's Royal Ambassador (Lefty) won the 1986 BCA National Specialty show. He is also a multiple Specialty show winner. Lefty is a son of Tyrol's Quintus Millitus and Hoogh's Bundle Buns.

*Am. Ch. Hoogh's
Stonehenge Sally.*

Ashbey.

*Am. Ch. Hoogh's
Crown Royal.*

Tatham.

Ch. Hoogh's Crown Royal (Tuffy) is jointly owned by Bob and Susan Rodenski and Bruce Smith, bred by Bruce Smith and Barbara McGlinchey. He is the father of Ch. Fidelis Kiss Me Kate, Ch. Fidelis Lord Gepp and Ch. Fidelis Mystical Merlin, who finished in three 5pt Specialty shows. Tuffy is by Ch. Hoogh's Royal Ambassador out of Ch. Hoogh's Stonehenge Sally.

Ch. Hoogh's Stonehenge Sally's successes in the show ring include Winners Bitch at 1985 BCA National Specialty weekend, Bulldog Club of Chicago, and Best of Winners at 1986 BCA Division 1 Specialty.

NEWCOMB
Owned by ROBERT AND BRENDA NEWCOMB
Ch. Newcomb's Desert Victory, bred, owned and handled by Robert and Brenda Newcomb, co-breeders Phil & Connie Booker, 'Victor' is one of those dogs that comes along very seldom in any breed. He has outstanding conformation combined with excellent health and topped off with a real show personality. He began his show career at the age of nine months, at the BCA National Show in Seattle. He was reserve Winners Dog and Best Puppy on the first day and Best of Winners for 5 pts and Best Puppy on the second day. He went on to win two more 5pt majors to finish his championship.

Victor and his litter sister, Ch. Newcomb's Desert Daisy, both finished their championships before they were a year old, and both went on to be Specialty Show BoB winners. With very limited showing Daisy won three large specialty shows and several BoS. Victor has won BoB at 26 specialty shows and BoS at the 1993 BCA National Show, which placed him among the very select group of BCA National Gallery winners.

Victor was honoured by the Pedigree dog food company as the top Bulldog for 1993, having defeated more Bulldogs than any other Bulldog for the year. Victor is by Ch. Newcomb's Magic Mac ex Ch. Stonehenge Xtra Peppermint.

*Am. Ch. Newcomb's
Desert Victory.*

TSAR
OWNED BY JAMES AND SOYA CARDELLO
This well-known New Hampshire kennel has produced many excellent, top-winning Bulldogs. Ch. Tsar's Manhattan of Norfield has won many BoB wins including BoB at the Long Island BC show in September 1993, and BoB at the BC of St. Louis, the second show of National Week 1993, over a record entry of three hundred and thirty-three, including seventy-three Specials. Manhattan is by Ch. Tsar's Maker's Mark out of Norfields Norma Jean, and was born July 7th 1991.

*Am. Ch. Tsar's Fat
Man's Finale, pictured
winning BoB at the
BCA National
Specialty, 1991.*

Callea.

Am. Ch. Tsar's Manhattan of Norfield, pictured winning BoB over a record entry at the Bulldog Club of St Louis, 1993.

Giacomo.

Ch. Tsar's Fat Man's Finale had many BoB wins to his credit, including BoB at the BC of Connecticut and BoB at the BC of New England, both in 1991, prior to his big National win at the BCA Specialty. Unfortunately he died on the flight home from the Nationals, ending what would have been an outstanding show career. He was one month short of his second birthday at the time. He is the sire of three champions, and his portrait is in the BCA National Gallery of Winners. His sire was Ch. Tsar's Call Me The Fat Man out of Bonnies Big Bad Bertha.

Ch. Tsar's Fabulous Moolah (Ch. Lebo's Horsefeathers – Tsar's Tinkerbell) won BoS at the 1987 BCA Specialty show – the first bitch in nineteen years to be awarded this honour from the regular classes. She finished her championship that day with a 5pt major.

Moolah is the dam of three champions and it is hoped that she will soon follow her dam into the BCA Brood Bitch Hall of Fame for having produced four or more Champions. Her portrait is in the BCA Gallery of Winners.

GLYNDEBOURNE
OWNED BY CLAIRE P. TOMLINSON

Claire Tomlinson is a Member of the BCA's Hall of Fame. She is the breeder of several top Specialty winners including Ch. Glyndebourne Royal Fanfare, a multiple Group and Best in Specialty show winner and a member of the BCA's Producers Hall of Fame. His progeny include seventeen champions and a BCA National Specialty Award of Merit winner.

Ch. Kozabull Glyndebourne Zeke is another multiple Group and Best in Specialty show winner and member of the BCA's Producers Hall of Fame. Zeke won the Award of Merit at the BCA National Specialty 1990 and has been awarded over 100 BoB wins.

Ch. Glyndebourne Baritone is a Group and multiple Best in Specialty show winner, including Best in Show at the BCA National Specialty 1992. Ch. Glyndebourne Impresaria is a member of the BCA's Producers Hall of Fame.

Am. Ch. Glyndebourne Royal Fanfare.

Klein.

CANADA

The first Bulldog recorded with the Canadian Kennel Club was registration no. 445 which simply states: Male. Name: Met. by Butch Skin (imp) owned by H.J. Leslie, Toronto. The next entry for the breed was no. 1236. Bitch. Name: Flash. August 10th 1887. Colour: Fallow. By Crib, dam Simter of Lions, owned by A.D. Stewart, Hamilton. Breeder Dr Bedell-Benison, Birmingham.

CANADIAN BREEDERS

One Canadian Bulldog breeder and exhibitor to have gained world-wide recognition is Joan Railton of the famous Taunton kennel. Joan had wanted a Bulldog for some time but her partner, with whom she owned a girls school, threatened to resign if she brought one home. However, in 1939 Joan had to ask her veterinary surgeon, Dr R.G. Cuthbert, to put down her thirteen-month old Newfoundland as he was becoming very bad-tempered; Dr Cuthbert lent

Can. Am. Ch. Taunton Grenadier, pictured in 1950, winning one of his many BIS awards, with his owner/breeder Joan Railton.

Joan a Bulldog that had been boarded with him and apparently abandoned.

The poor dog had obviously been a family pet because, when Joan arrived back at the school with him, it was lunch time and the girls were sitting at the dining-room tables. There was an empty chair and Nosey, as he had been christened, climbed up into it and behaved beautifully for the rest of the meal. Joan kept him for just a few months until his health gave out and he had to return to the vet's.

Joan started searching for another Bulldog and bought Westholme Monologue from a breeder on Vancouver Island. Monologue was shown and soon became a Canadian champion; so then began another hunt, this time for a suitable stud. It was Mona, as she was called, who introduced Joan to the USA dog scene.

In order to understand the relationship between Canadian and American Bulldogs the geography of North America has to be taken into consideration. The Rocky Mountain ranges run north to south and cut British Columbia and the Pacific coast of the USA off from the more eastern parts of the continent, thus encouraging breeders to travel south to the American kennels rather than over the Rockies to Alberta and Canadian provinces further

ABOVE: Joan Railton pictured after winning the Bulldog Club of America Championship Show in 1961, with Best of Winners Can. Am. Ch. Taunton Yemima (left) and her dam, Can. Am. Ch. Gatewood Miss Bar Baker, who was Best Opposite Sex.

RIGHT: Kamel Morovian Mainspring, imported from the UK in the 1950s for Reg Sparkes' famous Kamel kennel in Ontario.

Can. Ch. Joymuir Smirnoff Salty: Imported from Bob Dennett's UK kennel in 1979.

east. In looking for a stud dog for Mona, Joan met Gus and Lou Nelson who owned the well-known **Gatewood kennels of Seattle**, Washington. Mona was mated to a top stud there on three occasions, but without success.

Some years later when Dr and Mrs Saylor of Long Beach, California imported Eng. Ch. Kippax Fearnought, Joan took advantage of the Rocky Mountains and made the easy trip South to see him. Fearnought later went on to win Best in Show at the famous Westminster show.

Can. & Am. Ch. Taunton Brigadier was born in 1944. Around this time Reg Sparkes of the **Kamel kennel, Ontario** fame was the big name in Bulldogs in Canada. Many English breeders will remember Reg as a judge and as an importer into Canada of many of the dogs he met at the English shows. Reg was born in Bath, England   and donated the magnificent Kamel Trophy to the Bath and Western Counties Bulldog Club, UK. This trophy is competed for   annually in a special class confined to dogs bred by exhibitor.

Joan had a particularly good day when she entered Brigadier at a Bulldog specialty show in Alberta in April 1945, where Reg Sparkes awarded him Best of Breed. Later that day Brigadier was awarded Best in Show by Bill Pym, an all-breeds judge and president of the Canadian Kennel Club. In August of the same year Brigadier went Best in Show, all breeds, in Victoria, under the well-known dog man, Billy Oates.

Shortly after this Joan decided to retire Brigadier from the Canadian show ring as she had been elected the British Columbian director of the CKC. In the USA Brigadier went Best in Show, all breeds, at the Washington show in 1946 under judge A.W. Brockway, Chicago. Soon after this he completed his American championship. After Brigadier's retirement, his son, Can. & Am. Ch. Taunton Grenadier, continued his sire's winning ways, but died of bloat at the age of three.

At the Bulldog Club of America show held in 1961 at Portland, Washington, Am. & Can. Ch. Miss Bar Baker was Best Opposite Sex and her daughter, Can. Ch. Taunton Yemima, was Best of Winners. They were beaten by Dr E.M. Vardon's famous Am. & Can. Ch. Vardona Frosty Snowman.

In the summer of 1962 Joan fulfilled a long-held ambition, to go to England to purchase a bitch. Instead she returned with Hawkshope Angeline from Miss Peggy Hawkes and Dewrie Silver Cloud from John and Eirwen Davies. Both became Canadian champions. In 1979 Joan imported Joymuir Smirnoff Salty, bred by Mr M.C. Dennett of the UK. In due course Joan decided to breed her back to her sire, Eng. Ch. Aldridge Advent Gold, if arrangements could be made for the importation of frozen semen. Joan believes this was a first for Canada. Les Cotton, owner and breeder of Advent Gold, was most helpful and, after a great deal of red tape, this was accomplished. To the great disappointment of both Joan and her good friend and vet Dr Peter Woodyer, the breeding was unsuccessful.

Since moving to Nova Scotia in 1970 Joan has imported five bitches and two dogs from England and made Canadian champions of them all. The Taunton kennel presently houses two imports, ten-year-old Can. Ch. Hawkshope Fearless, a son of Eng. Ch. Merriveen Halcyon Daze, and Can. Ch. Kingrock Jingle Belle, a daughter of Eng. Ch. Kingrock Canis Pugnax.

Chapter Fourteen

THE BULLDOG WORLDWIDE

FRANCE

In the February of 1964, a lady called Madame de Bourdon, a breeder of Bulldogs, wrote to her friends: "I have the pleasure to announce that the Club du Bulldog Anglais was created yesterday."

The Bulldog Club of France came into existence a century after its British counterpart and grew from strength to strength in its early years. However, after the death of Madame de Bourdon, the club's founder, some time passed before her position was taken up by Madame Gautier. In October 1977 Georges Lacaud was elected president, a post he held until 1992. Helene Denis, who had been the secretary of the club for many years, was then elected president. Raymond Triquet, author of many books, the most famous being 'le Dictionnaire de la Cynophilie', has held the office of vice president since the club began.

The Club du Bulldog Anglais looks after the breed's development in France and also ensures that it is is promoted in a correct manner. Three times a year it publishes a magazine and organises an annual show, the 'Exposition Nationale d'Elevage', which gives breeders and judges an opportunity to check on the breed's development at close quarters.

During this show the dogs are carefully examined and also take part in temperament tests. Those who pass are awarded points on a scale system which ultimately adds value to the puppies they produce. The club also organises shows which are held in conjunction with all-breed shows. One of the club's main objectives is to keep its membership in close touch with each other, and to maintain a spirit of friendly co-operation. In 1993 the club had four hundred and thirty-eight members.

The popularity of the Bulldog in France has grown steadily from its early beginnings in 1969, with just two registrations for the year, to a healthy one hundred and sixty-nine registrations for 1993. Many of the dogs registered each year were imported from the UK and, unfortunately, some were only of pet quality, although enough good stock arrived to give the breed a firm foundation. Credit must also be given to the dedicated French breeders who were determined to see the Bulldog firmly established in their country.

The following is a list of Bulldog champions who have gained their French title in recent years. It is interesting to note that most of these were either imported from the UK or are progeny of these imports. However, over the years, several imports have also arrived in France from the United States and Holland and have played an important role in the breed's development.

CHAMPIONS OF FRANCE

1980	Thomas of Outdoors: owner Andre Leblond
1981	Olympe: owner Andre Leblond
1982	Tuffnuts Champers: owner Rene Boudon
1983	Jaylou's Beau Jangles: owners Helene Denis & M.T.Bertrand
	Sally Little Princess Di Isella: owner Chantel Julien
1984	Ocobo British Passion: owner Helene Denis
	Jaylou's Melodie: owner Helene Denis
1985	Beefeater Bulls Emerald Lady: owner Charles Semser
1986	Beefeater Bulls Eileen O'Grady: owner Mme Roosenboom
1987	Vicking Du Petit Yeti: owner Lucien Grolleau
1988	Merriveen Fleur Daze: owner Denis Hindie
	Thydeal Chance: owner Luciano Orsi
1989	Crazy Horse De Wounded Knee: owner Celine Bottussi
	Vicking Du Petit Yeti: owner Lucien Grolleau
	Beefeater Bulls Groomsport Baby: owner M.Daems
	Isidoor After Tacha: owner Marga Lockefer
	Thydeal Chance: owner Luciano Orsi
	Sandean Dead Lucky: owner Helene Denis
1990	Ocobo Royal Flag: owner Jules Lavaux
	Cindy Du Chemin Fleury: owner Jules Lavaux
	Anemone Des Monts D'Artois: owner Roselyne Vandamme
	Duke of Kent of the Water Regions: owner M.Schuurmans
	Antoinette De Benaval: owner Corinne Poisson
	Bonifacio's Fernando of Sandean: owner Helene Denis
1991	Boo's Apple Cider: owner Celine Bottussi
	Diamond J. De Wounded Knee: owner Joel Julou
1992	Winrice Che Bop: owner Corinne Poisson
	Jaylou's Brutus Maximus: owner Helene Denis
	Eaque Des Bulls Du Barnum: owner Mme Simon
1993	Fairy Tale Du Quarrylane Cottage: owner Helene Denis

INTERNATIONAL CHAMPIONS
(owned by French exhibitors)

Jaylou's Beau Jangles: owners Helene Denis & M.T.Bertrand
Ocobo British Passion: owner Helene Denis
Vicking Du Petit Yeti: owner Lucien Grolleau

Int. Ch. Ocobo British Passion, owned by Helene Denis, bred in the UK by Pat and Norman Davis. British Passion is a son of the famous Eng. Ch. Ocobo Skipper.

Fr. Ch. Merriveen Fleur Daze, owned by Denis Hindie. Fleur Daze is a daughter of Eng. Ch. Merriveen Happy Daze, and was bred in the UK by Pat Dellar.

Crazy Horse De Wounded Knee: owner Celine Bottussi
Ocobo Royal Flag: owner Jules Lavaux
Cindy Du Chemin Fleury: owner Jules Lavaux
Boo's Apple Cider: owner Celine Bottussi
Eaque Des Bulls Du Barnum: owner Mme Simon
Pickwick Quatty: owner Edwige Denis

In France the Bulldog Club exercises quite considerable control over its membership with regard to their breeding programme. The club is given this power by the French dog world's governing body, the Societe Centrale Canine, who in turn take their authority from the country's Ministrie de L'Agriculture.

Although the stud book is in the exclusive ownership of the SCC, the clubs have the right to control breeding by granting points to the stock on a scale system. The maximum points is six, and this gives the dog the title 'Reproducer d'Elite'. This denotes that this is a first-rate sire or dam; the title is only granted to those dogs and bitches who have produced more than five winners of an award equivalent to a CC.

At this present time very few have attained this high award:

> Int. Ch. Jaylou's Beau Jangles
> Int. Ch. Ocobo British Passion
> Int. Ch. Ocobo Royal Flag
> Int. Ch. Boo's Apple Cider
> Fr. Ch. Sandean Dead Lucky
> Fr. Ch. Bonifacio's Fernando of Sandean
> Int. Ch. Eaque Des Bulls Du Barnum

Bulldogs in French ownership have made quite an impact on the show scene in recent years. Int. Ch. Ocobo British Passion gained reserve Best in Show at the World Show in Amsterdam in 1985 from an entry of 10,000 dogs and more recently, in 1992, Fr. Ch. Bonifacio's Fernando of Sandean won BIS at the Longchamp show from an entry of 5,200 dogs (Longchamp is held in Paris and is the equivalent to the UK's Crufts).

Nowadays it is not unusual for a Bulldog to win a Group or even BIS at an all-breed show in France.

We must not forget the French breeders who have striven for improvement. One of the first was Andre Leblond, with the prefix **'du Domaine Des Drontes'** who decided to give up breeding Bulldogs some years ago when he found the work-load too much. M. Leblond is a respected all-round judge and spends much of his time travelling the world on judging engagements.

Helene Denis' prefix **'du Quarrylane Cottage'** is widely known. Helene is president of the Bulldog club and a respected judge of the breed. As the owner of Int. Ch. Ocobo British Passion and of Fr. Ch. Bonifacio's Fernando of Sandean, Helene has certainly made an impact on the breed, and she is the only person in Bulldogs in France to have been granted the title of 'Elevage Recommande' by the Societe Centrale Canine. This title is extremely hard to obtain and is reserved for breeders who consistently produce good stock, although this in itself is not sufficient, as the person's 'ethical manner' is also taken into account.

Among the kennels currently producing good stock are: Jules Lavaux's **'Bulls Du Barnum'**, Celine Bottussi's **'Wounded Knee'** and Brigitte Aviot's **'Des 4 Jeudis'**. But most Bulldog breeders in France are owners of small kennels with perhaps just one or two bitches producing the occasional litter.

FINLAND

The first Bulldogs registered in Finland appeared in The Finnish Kennel Club Calendar and Breed Book, Part One, dated 1889-1893:

No.250 Dog: Grogg
        Representative: K. Wiborg
        Breeder: Unknown
        Born: April 1890 English import
        Colour: Fawn with grey marks
        Sire: Unknown
        Dam: Unknown
        3rd prize at Helsinki 1892

No.251 Bitch: Tonny
        Owner: Riding teacher, C. Ducander, Helsinki
        Breeder: Unknown
        Born: 1890
        Colour: Brindle
        Sire: Unknown
        Dam: Unknown
        3rd prize Helsinki 1892

The first Bulldog breeder mentioned in this publication was Mr Gunnar Jack, towards the end of the 1800s, and the earliest registered kennel name, which was 'of Albion', appeared in the seventh edition of the Breed Book 1908-1911, in the ownership of Mr K.A. Hellman of Leppavaara.

However, by the time of the next edition, covering the period 1911-1913, there were twenty-two Bulldogs registered, fifteen dogs and seven bitches, four of which were English imports, one of which was:

        Name: Prinz Oak
        Breeder: Cutbert
        Born: November 14th 1908
        Sire: Solid Oak (grandfather of Ch. Oak Nana)
        Dam: Larfin Girl

Ninety Bulldogs were imported into Finland between 1911 and 1990, an average of one a year: of these, fifty-nine were imported from the UK. However, since 1988 the yearly average has risen to more than seven. English kennels which have played a major part in the breed's development in Finland are Bondabull, Outdoors, Kingrock, Baytor, Aldridge and Wencar.

During the war years of the forties no registrations for the breed appeared in the Breed Book and the 'old lines' disappeared. However, in 1945 Mrs Ulla Segerstrom's famous **'Ullah's'** kennel became established in Helsinki, producing such well-known dogs as SF Ch. Ullah's Boomerang and Ullah's Attraction. Attraction was the first Bulldog owned by Dr & Mrs Kuusisto, who were founder members of the Bulldog Club of Finland and a great

Fin. Ch. Young Count Kingrock, a son of Eng. Ch. Kingrock Canis Pugnax, with owner Helena Hyvonen.

Fin. Ch. Madonna: Finland's top winning Bulldog bitch in 1988, 1989 and 1990. Owned by Helena and Ari Hyvonen, bred by Ari Hyvonen and A. Peramaki.

Black Hope Lady-Killer and her litter sister Black Hope Little-Lisa, sired by Fin. and Est. Ch. Tretun Bustersam of Kingrock out of Kingrock Tiger Lily.

driving force in those early days. Mrs Paula Vuori of the **'Kekale'** affix started her Bulldog kennel in 1953 and produced many Finnish champions over a period of twenty years, including the well-known SF Ch. Kekale Jankka. Mrs Vuori imported from the UK SF Ch. Chiansline Chevalier Jakkara from John and Sheila Alcock. Jakkara was sired by Wintersmoon Jason ex Sospan Princess of Henlobeds.

Others kennels which have been actively involved in the breed include:

Muorinmoision, owned by Mrs Ritva Vesa-Patokorpi and founded in July 1963, and **Tuhkiala,** which is owned by Mrs Leena Tuhkanen, established in September 1965. In 1969 the Tuhkiala kennel imported Thydeal Stroller from Harold Hayball (UK). Stroller was sired by Baytor Zircon Solo ex Thydeal Audiozone and went on to become an Int. & Scandinavian champion. He was the sire of many champions including SF Ch. Tuhkiala Putinki.

Meriwia is owned by Seppo Mattila, who started in the breed in 1978 and imported Bondabull Samuel from Bob Wain (UK). Samuel was by Ch. Outdoors Jubilant ex Bondabull Angel Delight and went on to gain his SF and Norwegian titles. He was also the top Bulldog in Finland in 1984. His champion progeny include Int. & Scandinavian Ch. Victorville.

Unelman, owned by Jari Laakso. This leading kennel, based on English imports, has come to the fore in recent years. Jari Laakso imported Bondabull Raspberry from her UK breeder, Bob Wain, in 1985. She was sired by Ch. Broomwick Barrowboy of the Regions ex Bondabull Pretty Prudence. Raspberry's daughter, Unelman Cloudberry, became an SF Ch. and her father was the UK import Int. and Scandinavian Ch. Portfield Buster's Boy.

Aldridge Andiamo: The dog CC winner at the 1993 Vantaa Show, judged by Chris Thomas. Owned by Larse Numni and Arja Harri, bred in the UK by Les and Ellen Cotton.

Cloudberry was mated to UK import Doughboy of the Regions and produced several winners, including SF Ch. Unelman Cock of the Walk, who in turn sired many Finnish champions.

Harrenhaus, owned by Mrs Arja Harri-Aallas who imported from the UK Isgraig Snow Prince, who went on to become a SF Ch. and became the top winning Bulldog in Finland for 1989 and 1990.

Admirabull, owned by Mrs Christine Mattila. In 1984 this kennel imported from the UK Bondabull Oliver Twist, who went on to gain his Int., Scandinavian and Finnish W-86 titles. He was sired by Ch. Outdoors Jubilant ex Bondabull Buxteds Baby. In 1985 Mrs Mattila imported a bitch from Mrs Terry Brunton (UK), Sandean British Spirit, born in 1985 by Sandean Sweet William ex Outdoors Daddy's Girl at Sandean. British Spirit went on to become a SF and Swedish Ch. She was mated to Int. and Scandinavian Ch. Edgewick Fearnought, producing the well-known SF and S. Ch. Admirabull Abracadabra, the top winning Bulldog in Finland in 1988.

Black Hope, owned by Ari and Helena Hyvonen, a young couple who have made quite an impact on the Finnish Bulldog scene in recent years. They started their kennel in 1987, and in 1989 bred SF Ch. Black Hope Ballerina, sired by SF and S Ch. Admirabull Abracadabra ex SF Ch. Madonna. Black Hope Ballerina was Finland's top producing bitch for 1992 and 1993. In 1989 they imported from us SF Ch. Kingrock Stonewall Jackson, sired by Ch. Kingrock Captain Christian ex Lamb Chop of Kingrock. Jackson was the sire of many

Fin. Ch. Beefeater Bulls Hogans Hero, bred by Ann van den Heuvel-Cowan, owned by Hannu Palo-oja.

Finnish champions. In 1990 Helena and Ari imported Tretun Bustersam of Kingrock from the UK. Bustersam was bred by Anne Higginbottom and sired by Int. and Nordic Ch. Kingrock Buster ex Rockytop Guinevere of Tretun. Bustersam gained the titles SF and Est. Ch., EUJW-91, Finnish Winner 92-93, Estonia Winner 93. He was the top winning Bulldog of Finland in 1991 and 1992 and also the country's top stud dog for 1993, having sired many champions. This kennel's latest import, again from our kennel, Young Count Kingrock, has recently gained his Finnish title.

The Bulldog Club of Finland was founded on November 10th 1971 and was officially registered by the Finnish Kennel Club on February 23rd 1972. In 1989 the Club held its first official show, where the judge, Mrs Carol Newman (UK), awarded Best in Show to SF and S. Ch. Admirabull Abracadabra.

Int. and Nordic Ch. Edgewick Fearnowt.

SWEDEN

Since the beginning of 1980, Bulldogs have had great success in the show rings of Sweden. This coincided with the importation of new bloodlines from the UK. Although it is the dogs who tend to take the limelight, the importation of sound, healthy bitches is equally important. At the beginning of the 1980s Sw. Ch. Kingrock Tudor Flower, bred by myself, acquitted herself well not only in the show ring but as progenitor of several winning lines. During the mid '80s two top-winning Bulldogs were being campaigned at the same time, Ulla Segerstrom's Eng. and Sw. Ch. Tyegarth Lucifer, who was top Bulldog and top in the utility group for 1985, and Ove Germundsson's Sw. Ch. Edgewick Fearnowt, who was the top Bulldog and top in the utility group for 1986, 1987 and 1988.

Eng. Int. & Nordic Ch. Kingrock Buster had a extremely successful stay with Ove Germundsson during the late Eighties. Buster had won BIS at the Junior Bulldog Club show and the CC and BoB under Joe Braddon at the Birmingham championship show before leaving the UK to be campaigned in Scandinavia. He then went on to win his Swedish, Norwegian, Finnish, Nordic and International titles, picking up group and BIS wins along the way. In 1990 Buster returned to the UK where he won a further two CCs, thereby attaining his UK championship. Buster's photograph, taken when he was nine-and-a-half years of age, appears on the front cover of this book, and he is now enjoying his retirement at my home. 1989 saw the birth of a new star on the Swedish show scene, Sw. Ch. Extrems Jimjams Jezebel, by Sw. Ch. Edgewick Fearnowt ex Sw. Ch. Sunnyhill Birget, was the top winning Bulldog, top utility group winner and the third top winning dog, all breeds, in Sweden for 1989. Birget was mated to the UK import, Sw. Ch. Sibley Jameson at Cidelott,

Int. Sw. Nor. Ch.
Extrems Jimjams
Jezebel.

which produced a litter of five puppies. The puppy retained by breeder Ove Germundsson became   Sw. Ch. Extrems Ovation of Osyth.

Ovation won 34 CCs, 31 BoBs, 24 groups, 18 Best in Shows and became the top winning dog of all breeds in Sweden for 1992 – the first time a Swedish-born Bulldog had achieved this title.

*Int. Sw. Nor. Ch.
Extrems Ovation of
Osyth, with
owner/breeder Ove
Germundsson.*

HOLLAND

The first bulldog to be registered at the Dutch Kennel Club was Leuven's Young Baron, born in 1888 and registered in 1892, KC no. 171. His sire was Young Baron KS.B. 18133 and his dam Noisy Girl, breeder J.F. Preeze, UK. Baron was owned by the famous and well-respected author of books on all breeds of dogs, Graaf van Bylandt, and won two first prizes at the International show held at   Scheveningen in 1892.

The first litter of bulldogs officially registered at the Dutch KC was in 1893, bred by Graaf van Bylandt. The first recognised Bulldog breed club was founded in 1907. However, due to turmoil caused by the two World Wars, most of the historical documentation for the first half of this century has been lost.

The most famous bulldog of the 1950s was Dutch Ch. Bonzo of Bulldene. Bonzo was born in England on June 8th 1953, sired by Prince of Woodgate, dam Beauty of Bulldene, and imported to Holland by Mr J.J.Fris. In 1954 Bonzo won the Amsterdam Winner's title when he was just ten months old. He then went on to take the Amsterdam Winner's title six times and won five Best in Shows, a record still unbeaten to this day.

1960 was the year for another famous Dutch dog to make an appearance – Dutch Ch. Bobo from the **Ja-Gri** kennels, a son of Bonzo, bred by the Jansens, who owned the leading kennel of the 1960s. Bobo took the Amsterdam winner's title in 1960 and 1961, and won four BIS, including BIS at the Amsterdam Winners show of 1961. The last litter born at the Ja-Gri kennel was in 1979, which produced Dutch Ch. Donna of the Ja-Gri, making her the last of the six champions bred by this kennel.

In the late 1970s and early 1980s Goldenrun of the Seven Seas, Amsterdam winner 1980, bred by Mrs van de Zee, really left his mark on the breed in Holland, being the sire of five champions and many other CC winners. One of his great features was his width of underjaw and strength of foreface, which can still be found in many of his progeny today. Goldenrun was the first bulldog on the Continent to be born from frozen semen: his sire was the legendary English Ch. Aldridge Advent Gold. From the Seven Seas kennel came also Dutch Ch. Udine of the Seven Seas and Dutch Ch. Paddles of the Seven Seas.

Ann van den Heuvel-Cowan's **Beefeater Bulls** affix is behind the breeding of many winning Continental kennels but nowhere more so than in the Netherlands. In 1980 the litter sisters Dutch Ch. Beefeater Bulls Banshee Baby, Amsterdam winner 1984, and Dutch Ch. Beefeater Bulls Blarny's Kiss, Amsterdam junior winner 1981, were born. These litter sisters won many CCs and BIS awards between them. Banshee Baby was the first bulldog bitch ever to win groups in Holland at championship shows. She was also the dam of Multi-champion and group-winning Beefeater Bulls Danny Boy, Italian and Int. Ch. Beefeater Bulls Finnagan Finn and the all-breed BIS winning Multi-Ch. Beefeater Bulls Finney O'Toole.

Dutch Ch. Beefeater Bulls Blarny's Kiss was the dam of four champions in one litter: Dutch Ch. Beefeater Bulls Evermore Irish, Amsterdam winner 1986 and group winner the same year (also, in 1985, the first Bulldog to go reserve dog all-breeds in the Netherlands);

The Dutch Bulldog and French Bulldog Club 1985. BIS line-up (left to right): BOS Int. Ch. Beefeater Bulls Blarny's Kiss, handled by owner/breeder Ann van den Heuvel-Cowan, the judge is English breed specialist Dora Wakefield, and BIS is the famous Int. Ch. Blighty's Nero, handled by his owner Gert-Jan Wagermans, bred by Tony Williams.

Dutch Ch. Beefeater-Bulls Got To Be Irish, owned by Ann Peperkamp. Sired by Doughboy of the Regions (UK import) out of Beefeater Bulls Etta Murphy.

South African and Lux. Ch. Roseneath Quest, owned by Ann van den Heuvel-Cowan.

Dutch Ch. Beefeater Bulls Eniskillen Hero, group winner; French Ch. Beefeater Bulls Emerald Lady, a BIS winner; and Dutch Ch. Beefeater Bulls Eileen O'Grady.

All of the Beefeater champions of today, twelve to date, are bred as closely as possible to Dutch Ch. Beefeater Bulls Blarny's Kiss. The Beefeater kennels have imported stud dogs from the UK. One of these, Doughboy of the Regions, the sire of two British champions, also sired seven champions on the Continent including the top winning Bulldog to date, Multi and World Ch. 1989 Beefeater Bulls Groomsport Baby.

Dutch Ch. Elroston Colonial Boy JW 1989 BIS winner was imported from Australia. He has sired four champions to date and many CC winners, including Dutch Ch. Australian Boy

LEFT: Int. Ch. Beefeater Bulls Finney O'Toole: Bulldog of the Year 1987 and BIS All Breeds, San Remo 1989.

BELOW: Int. Ch. Romakome Admiral O'Toole: Bulldog of the Year 1991 and 1992.

van de Boefjes, who went BIS at the largest event ever organised for Bulldogs on the Continent, with two hundred and forty-eight entries.

Colonial Boy was followed by the South African import, World Champion 1991, JW 1990 Roseneath Quest. Quest is the sire of many CC winners today, including the BIS winner at the Belgian club show 1993, the BIS winner of the Dutch club show 1993 and the top winning Twinkle Star of the Royal Club, sired by Quest ex Beefeater Bulls Hester O'Mally.

In the mid 1980s Rob and Mary Kostor started their **Romakome** kennel. They had great success with their first Bulldog, Dutch Ch. Beefeater Bulls Enniskillen Hero, who was followed by Multi Ch. Beefeater Bulls Finney O'Toole. These dogs, mated to imported bitches from the UK, including a Sandean from Mrs Terry Brunton's famous kennel, have produced champions in both Holland and Italy.

The Bulldog has become one of Holland's most popular breeds – between sixty-nine and ninety puppies are registered monthly at the Dutch KC, putting the breed into the top twenty in Holland.

SOUTH AFRICA

South Africa is another country in which the Bulldog has flourished for more than a century. The first Bulldog registered with the South African Kennel Club, the forerunner of today's Kennel Union of South Africa, was in 1891, when Billy, owned by Mr C. Knight, appeared as entry No. 42 on the first page of the handwritten register, dated September 11th of that year. No further Bulldogs were registered with the South African Kennel Club until March 1906 when George Welch registered his Fairplay, by Woodcote out of Monella. Later that

S.A. Ch. Roseneath Devlin: A multiple BIS winner, owned and bred by George and Julia van Rooyen.

S.A. Ch. Lerohan Emile of Ravenmoor: BOB at the Transvaal Utility Club Show 1993. Owned by Percy and Margaret Bevan.

year he registered Brighton Dot, by Hazelmore Prince out of Cherry Girl.

The South African Bulldog Club was founded by Dr Currie in September 1908 and staged its first show on February 20th 1909. From one class of twelve Bulldogs the winners were: Plantiflora, Miss Cribb, White Knight and reserve, Sterling. In 1913 Dr Currie stood down as chairman in favour of Mr Gregson who, with the assistance of the club's first secretary, George Wheelwrite and his committee organised their first championship show on August 4th 1913. The club's second championship show was held on October 5th 1914. During the Great War, club activities were confined to one meeting a year. After the war the SABC, under the chairmanship of Mr W.H. Furnival, assisted with the re-organisation of the SAKC, only to be severely impeded once again, this time due to the state of martial law which existed during 1921 and 1922 as a result of the rebellion.

In 1923 a branch of the SABC was started in Cape Town and flourished under the sponsorship of Mrs Given Wilson. In July 1927 this branch became the Cape Bulldog Club. During this year the SABC held its third championship show. For this event a solid silver trophy was purchased for one hundred guineas (£105), hence the name 'The Hundred Guinea Cup'. The first winner of this prestigious trophy was Mrs J.H. Whiteley's Lady Douglas of Burradro.

Due to the country's financial difficulties during the years 1931-1933, membership of the SABC suffered badly, although match-meetings were occasionally held. Mr J. McGowan judged at one in April 1933, and placed dogs called Pugilistrian Wanglevale, Bondi Bradman, Bilton of Burradoo and Bill Riley.

S.A. Ch. Clarendon Challenger of Kingrock: Imported from the Kingrock kennel in the UK by Mr H.J. van der Merwe, owner of the Mervander kennel. A son of Int. Ch. Kingrock Buster, bred by Celia Campbell, Challenger was a consistent winner during the early 1990s and an influential sire.

S.A. Ch. Roseneath Eustone with some of the trophies and rosettes he amassed during one show season. Eustone is not only the top winning Bulldog of all time in South Africa, but also the top Champion producing sire of all time in South Africa.

In 1939 the East Rand Bulldog Club was founded, although strongly objected to by the SABC; this view was later reconsidered and a gold medal was presented to the new club at a cost of £2.17s.6d.

By 1940 the Second World War was well under way and took its toll on the younger enthusiasts. Blazeaway Springbok Warrior and Knocknashie Nina, owned by Mrs. Johnson, and Highgate Brown Bess, owned by Mr B.L. Vogelnest, were all winners at shows held during 1941-1943 in aid of war funds.

Several UK judges have officiated at SABC shows, the first being Arthur Westlake in 1969, followed by Len Doidge 1972, John Alcock 1974, Harold Hayball 1975, Arthur Westlake 1976 and Arthur Braithwaite in 1977. In June 1961 a medallion was received by the SABC from the Bath and Western Counties Bulldog Club, England, to be awarded for Best in Show.

In the early 1950s the famous **Goldfields** kennel belonging to Mr and Mrs J.A. Erasmus produced the legendary SA Ch. Goldfields Royal Flush, by Goldfields Zulu Warrior out of Goldfields Snow White. Another dog from this kennel, Goldfields Conqueror of Camwood, along with Tobruks Lunda Lou, formed the foundation stock for Di Wood's **Camwood** kennel. Both of these dogs went on to become champions and then produced many winning progeny including SA Ch. Brutus Beautiful, SA Ch. Red Sensation and SA Ch. Dream Boat Judy.

The **Mont Nora** kennel, belonging to George and Liz Harding, was established in 1950 and produced many champions, the most famous being SA Ch. Jealousy and SA Ch. Golden Dandy.

By the mid 1960s several more kennels were starting to make an impact on the breed, including such well-known names as Martha Taljaard, with her **Talies** kennel, which imported Bettebus Ben Peppis and Bettebus Miss Yankee from the USA in 1977, both becoming champions in 1978. Another of Martha's USA imports was Brookhollow Mark Nassan from Ernie Hubbard's famous kennel.

A puppy from the famous Talies kennel, La Mertsch's Playboy of Talies, was to form the foundation for what was to become another top producing line, the **Suca** kennel of Susan Visser and Kitty Pieterse. This kennel has bred thirty Bulldog champions, a truly great achievement.

The **Garlise** kennel produced some exceptional litters, including a litter of nine by SA Ch. Myras Sam of Jacozaan, from which seven became champions. SA Ch. Garlise Marysa was retained from this litter and when she was mated to SA Ch. Talies Demos of Anscha, produced a litter of which six became champions.

Mr & Mrs D. Rorke's **Tullamore** kennel had many well-known winners including the UK import SA Ch. Thatchway Cavalier of Tullamore, bred in 1969 by Claude and Magda Bannister.

The **Rockcliffe** affix of Bill & Lorna Lawlor was also becoming well established at this time. Bill Lawlor was a respected international judge, well-known to Bulldoggers in the UK. The Rockcliffe foundation stock was imported from Harold & Audie Hayball's Thydeal kennel, UK, the most famous being SA Ch. Rockcliffe's Thydeal Audacious who gained his title on November 10th 1975. Audacious was the sire of many champions as well as a great

*S.A. Ch.
Roseneath Fame.*

showman. He was awarded Best in Show at the Northern Transvaal KC all-breed show in 1977 from an entry of some one thousand five hundred dogs. Over the years this kennel imported ten Bulldogs, including Thydeal Prospect Pleases, Thydeal Endeavour and Unique of Thydeal. They also imported SA Ch. Outdoors Jonathan of Maidenhayne from George and Dora Wakefield's famous UK kennel. Jonathan was Best in Show at the Cape Bulldog Club's Jubilee Show in 1982.

At the beginning of the 1970s another world famous kennel was beginning to emerge, the **Roseneath** affix of George and Julia van Rooyen. This kennel's achievements are legendary, with twenty-two homebred champions, including South Africa's top sire of all time SA Ch. Roseneath Eustone, with sixteen champion progeny. As well as being a great sire, Eustone was a great show dog and in 1987 won the Dogmor Dog of the Year from an entry of two thousand five hundred. This kennel also owned and bred the top dam of all time, SA Ch. Roseneath Kahlua, the dam of seven champions, although Roseneath Sovrani ran her close by producing no fewer than six champions in one litter; their sire was SA Ch. Roseneath Jubilee.

The Roseneath kennel has imported nine Bulldogs, six from the USA, including SA Ch. Lebo's Dallas and SA Ch. Mapo's Maharani, two from the famous Beefeater Bulls kennel of the Netherlands, and one, Kingrock Field Marshall, from the UK.

The **Anscha** kennel of Schalk & Ansie Joubert became well established in the 1970s with SA Ch. Anscha Liza winning Best in Show at the Northern Transvaal BC championship show in 1978 and 1979.

In more recent years other kennels have come to the fore, including the **Sezer** kennel of Shirley and Arthur Seef who are regular visitors to the UK. This kennel has imported several dogs including Am. Ch. Dingmans Ernesto of Sezer from the USA and Clarendon Swashbuckler of Sezer, Clarendon Prize Asset of Sezer and Tretun Miss Honeysuckle from

*S..A. Ch.
Ravenmoor Jock,
owned and bred by
Percy and Margaret
Bevan.*

the UK. This kennel has produced many top winners, including the lovely SA Ch. Sezer's Nickle.

Another kennel to have made an impact on the breed in recent times is the **Mervander** affix of Mr H.J. van der Merwe. Among this kennel's well-known imports are SA Ch. Clarendon Challenger of Kingrock and Clarendon Mervander Dr Roy of Kingrock, both bred in the UK by Celia Campbell.

These kennels would be considered large by UK standards and, at the SABC championship show held in 1993 and judged by Ann van den Heuvel-Cowan from Holland, the Sezer kennel had ten dogs entered, while the Mervanders sported an entry of fourteen, just pipping the Roseneath's entry of thirteen.

Perhaps surprisingly, in 1993 the Bulldog was the third most popular breed in South Africa, with one thousand seven hundred and fifty registrations for the year. With Staffordshire Bull Terriers in first place and Bull Terriers in second place, the British bull breeds certainly seem to be assured of a lasting future in this country.

AUSTRALIA

Bulldogs first made their appearance on the Australian show scene during the 1870s. The careful selection of imports, accompanied by dedicated line-breeding programmes, have kept the Bulldog flag flying in the eight states and territories of this country.

*Aust. Ch. Chajen
Chivers Regal.*

In the 1890s there were several Bulldogs being exhibited in New South Wales, Queensland and Victoria. At the turn of the century the human population had a dramatic increase, mostly due to English immigrants eager to "start afresh" in this new unblemished country. Many Bulldogs accompanied their owners on the long and tedious voyage, providing sound foundation stock.

In 1892 Mr Cyril F.W. Jackson, a committee member of the Bulldog Club Incorporated, visited Australia and commented most favourably about the stock already in the country. Only two English champions have ever been imported into Australia – Broadford Amethyst and, some years later, Broadford Joan.

In Victoria, Mr and Mrs Len King imported Wise Guy of Wiggin and Kippax Rosie. Wise Guy was by Ch. Maelor Solarium out of the outstanding Ch. Easter Sensation of Wiggin. Sparingly used at stud, Wise Guy produced a top winner in Mr and Mrs Clauseen's Ch. Melvic Resolution, who was not only a top winning show dog, but an extremely prolific sire.

In more recent times there have been many commendable Bulldog imports. Several of these were imported by the **Wybong** kennel, including Aust. Ch. Portfield Monarch, Aust. Ch. Churinga Hesajimmy of Mellea and Aust. Ch. Brumigum Jessica Greg.

Craigrossie kennels in Melbourne have also imported dogs from the UK, including Aust. Ch. Merriveen Sno Flint, Aust. Ch. Kingrock Mr Angus and Kingrock Adam.

Elroston kennels have also played a part in an attempt to strengthen the breed, by introducing four UK imports: Aust. Ch. Ghezirah Bill Sykes of Ocobo, Aust. Ch. Ocobo Truly Royal, Aust. Ch. Ocobo China Doll, and Mr Dickens at Tretun. Over the years there have been quite a few breeders from all parts of Australia who have helped the Bulldog cause in one way or another, but mainly by bringing in fresh blood lines, thus creating a new gene pool with which to work.

Aust. Ch. Craigrossie Tommy Tucker, handled by co-owner Neil Stone.

Bulldogs in Australia's most populous State, New South Wales, have for many years enjoyed the strong support of loyal enthusiasts.

The longest established Bulldog kennel currently in operation is the **Kama** kennel belonging to Mrs Dulcie Partridge of Sydney. Many grand specimens have joined the ranks of a seemingly endless list of champions produced by this kennel, the product of a lifetime's devotion to the breed. Aust. Champions Kama Just Leroy, Miss Melony and Hush Puppy are but three of many. Gordon and Roma Long's **Donallen** kennel have, over the years, provided an abundant array of meritorious representatives, including Aust. Ch. Donallen Regal Lass, Aust. Ch. Donallen Hud, and probably the most famous of all, Aust. Ch. Donallen Lord Stuart, owned and expertly presented by Tracy Fox. Lord Stuart's charismatic ring manner and comely appearance launched him upon a winning spree that received some of the highest accolades. His son, Aust. Ch. Rocky Rambo, although not in the same league as his sire, was still quite an achiever and became a well-known celebrity nationwide, with his many appearances in television commercials.

The British Bulldog club of NSW has for quite some time been efficiently run by the owners of the **Chajen** kennel, Charles and Jean Turton. There have been quite a few memorable Chajen champions. One particularly stunning bitch was Aust. Ch. Chajen Devilish Mary, who gained remarkable success. Other champions of note are Chajen The

*Aust. Ch. Shyola
Tuppeny Doll.*

*Aust. Ch. Lyden
Madeira M'Dear.*

Boss, Glamour Girl and Chivers Regal. The city of Newcastle is home to several devoted
Bulldog fanciers. One such couple are George and Elizabeth Hoawerth, who began breeding
Bulldogs in 1976 under the **Nonparell** prefix, forging a very strong and distinct bitch line.
Aust. Champions Nonparell Lady Sarah, Maggie Thatch and Lady Leah were bitches of true
quality. However, their most eminent representative without a doubt was the lovely Aust.
Ch. Nonparell Miss Emmylou. Aside from her exceptional prowess as a show bitch, she
produced a chain of champions both at home and abroad.

A relative newcomer, Ms Susan Butler, with her **Oushiinu** Bulldog kennel, has
accomplished a great deal in the show ring, starting off with a dog called Aust. Ch. Wybong

*Aust. Ch. Donallen
Radiant Girl.*

*Aust. Ch. Donallen
Lord Stuart.*

Pied Piper. She subsequently used the top sire Aust. Ch. Elroston Mr Sandman, producing Aust. Champions Oushiinu Charlie Brown, a prominent BOB, Group and BIS winner, Oushiinu Laurel Lea and Oushiinu Annabelle, to name but a few.

Nestled among the vineyards of the Hunter Valley in the little town of Cessnock are the **Wybong** and **Soraya** kennels, owned by Wes Stacey. Although not as often seen in the show ring as was once the case, there have been several praiseworthy representatives carrying these kennel names over the years. The most prominent of all was Aust. Ch. Wybong Just Hooper, a truly remarkable dog whose show career is legendary, followed closely by Aust. Ch. Soraya Democrat.

*Aust. Ch.
Nonparell Miss
Emmylou.*

Further north in the countryside, the family team of Norman, Meryl and Howard Randell run the well-known **Elroston** kennel. Since the late 1970s Elroston have notched up seventeen champions, twelve of which were homebred, including Elroston Jungle Boy, Miss Hanky Panky, The Outlaw, Elroston Mr Terrific, Dutch Ch. Elroston Colonial Boy and the most famous, Aust. Ch. Elroston Mr Sandman, one of Australia's top winning Bulldogs of all time, in addition to siring a multitude of champions.

In the sunny state of Queensland, Reg and Lorraine Collins' **Reglor** Bulldogs are no strangers to the limelight. Aust. Ch. Reglor Lady Fergie won BIS under breed specialist Mrs Ann van den Heuval of Holland. Aust. Ch. Reglor Lady Lynette and Lady Sarah are just two of many other delightful bitches from this kennel.

In its day the **Saxondale** kennel, owned by Herb and Joan Field, held the Bulldog banner high with such dogs as Aust. Ch. Saxondale Krista Dan, Aust. Ch. Saxondale Ace Attack and Saxondale Royal Command. These names are to be found behind many of the big winners in Australia today.

Val and Kevin Williams, **Dontoro**, worked in close association with both the Saxondale and Elroston kennels to produce many champions. Likewise, Bev O'Hara's **Lyden** kennel has teamed up with the Craigrossie contingent of Melbourne to consistently breed quality stock, including Aust. Ch. Lyden Master Godfrey and Lyden Madeira M'dear.

From the state of Victoria comes the **Craigrossie** kennel owned by the dedicated team of

Eric Healey, Neil Stone and David Grebbin. This kennel has achieved a great deal of well-deserved success and has made quite an impact on the breed. Such dogs as Aust. Ch. Craigrossie Tommy Tucker and Aust. Ch. Craigrossie Finnius Fog, head the register of consistent winners accredited to this partnership. Their UK imports from the Merriveen and Kingrock kennels have done well in the show ring.

For many years the Bulldog Club of Victoria has been lucky enough to have Bill and Hazel O'Heir at its helm. The O'Heirs' **Lyndhaze** Bulldogs have received numerous honours, with winners such as Aust. Ch. Lyndhaze Dr Doolittle and Aust. Ch. Lyndhaze The General.

The city of Adelaide in South Australia is home to the **Shyola** kennel, owned by Faith and Richard Barry, who for many years have procured quite an array of remarkable achievers with the likes of Aust. Ch. Shyola Dilla, Penelope and Aphelia. Aust. Ch. Shyola Tuppeny Doll was another most outstanding bitch, enticing many a judge with her captivating appearance. She was accorded the ultimate honour at Australia's first Bulldog National show under breed specialist judge Mrs Sheila Alcock.

On the apple isle of Tasmania the Chan family's **Snobul** kennel is doing extremely well, rejuvenating interest among the other Bulldoggers of that State. Just a few of the Chan's big winners are Aust. Ch's. Snobul Dream Lover, Snobul Bonny Bess and Snobul Dream Royal.

Although Western Australia is somewhat isolated, due to the vastness of the country, their Bulldog club has been fortunate to have Ken Winter, Lenore Walsham and Brad Sinnatamby as members, doing their best to make sure the breed continues to flourish. One very devoted fancier, Mrs Betty Killerby, worked tirelessly for the club, doing her utmost to revitalise interest in Bulldogs among the canine fraternity of Western Australia. Her Aust. Ch. Oushiuu Eskimo Lad achieved considerable success.

ADVERTISING SECTION

BULLDOG BREEDERS' DIRECTORY

TYMARO BULLDOGS

R. L. & M. J. PENFOLD
2 Hawthorne Road, High Wycombe, Bucks. HP13 7EP
Tel: 01494-534451

TYMARO TRIP
Fawn & White. 28.2.91. Championship & Open Show winner

TYMARO TENDER TOUCH
Red & White. 22.7.94. Pictured at 8 weeks

Gwenstan Bulldogs

Quality puppies available at times.
Callers welcome at any time
by request to Mrs G. E. Biddle-Edwards.
(Licensed Kennels)

**The home of HAPPY BULLDOGS . . . I breed for love of the breed,
not for financial gain. I breed few litters each year,
but they are of GOOD QUALITY**

GWENDOLINE BIDDLE-EDWARDS
89 High Street, Upwood, Huntingdon, Cambs. PE17 1 QE
Telephone: Ramsey (01487) 814331

KINGROCK BULLDOGS
&
FRENCH BULLDOGS

To clarify the difference between a French and English Bulldog here is a
photograph of the French Bulldog
"English and American Champion Kingrock Poppyseed"
owned and bred by Chris Thomas and Graham Godfrey.

The French Bulldog is approximately half the weight of his English cousin.

Puppies of both breeds occasionally available.

Enquiries to : Meadow Cottage, Hendreforgan, Tonyrefail,
Mid-Glamorgan, CF39 8YB. United Kingdom.
Telephone & Fax 01443 672374

The Northern Bulldog Club

Founded 1933

Ten good reasons why you should be a member of this club

1. We were founded by working men, for the working man (the backbone of the breed).
2. This club welcomes all members old and new.
3. Help and advice freely and willingly given.
4. Our committee strives to please all our members and exhibitors.
5. We run two open shows each year.
6. We run a championship show every other year.
7. We are one of the few clubs still holding puppy competitions annually with four of our coveted solid silver medals on offer.
8. Our shows are based on low entry fees and good prize money given.
9. We are one of the few clubs to hold regular monthly meetings open to all members.
10. Members' subscriptions held low: £2 single and £3 joint membership.

Why not join us for a warm "Northern" welcome

For more information contact:

Hon. Secretary, Mr Fred Haynes, 129 Sunnyside Road, Droylsden, Manchester M43 7GF.   Tel: 0161 301 4227

Bulldog Club of Wales

President:
CHRIS THOMAS

HON. SECRETARY
MR J. LANE
16 WAUN FACH
PENTWYN
CARDIFF
CF2 7BA
TEL: 01 222 734631

NEW MEMBERS ALWAYS WELCOME.

PLEASE CONTACT THE HON. SECRETARY.

NOW AVAILABLE FOR
USE ON VIDEO
MACHINES OUTSIDE
THE USA AT
A SENSIBLE PRICE . . .

THE AKC VIDEO COLLECTION

Professionally written and narrated, and produced to the highest standards, the American Kennel Club Video Collection offers a complete guide to more than 70 breeds, based on the AKC Breed Standard. The Bulldog is featured in the series. Please order Code VT12. Also featured: *Dogsteps,* the famous and influential study of canine structure and movement (VT 67) and *Gait – Observing Dogs in Motion* (VT 63) which utilises a wide selection of breeds

Order from Ringpress Books, PO Box 8, Lydney, Gloucestershire, GL15 6YD, United Kingdom
Price: £17.50 including post and packing. Outside the UK: £20
Dogsteps: £25. Outside UK: £27.50